ANDREW MCCREA'S

American Countryside

Where Does Lost Luggage Go?

AND OTHER INSPIRING STORIES
FROM ACROSS THE LAND

♛
**BLAKE
& KING**
Maysville, Missouri

To order additional copies, contact Blake and King Publishers at:
5650 Berlin Road
Maysville, MO 64469

Publisher's Cataloging-in-Publication Data
McCrea, Andrew
       American countryside : where does lost luggage go? : inspiring stories from across the land / Andrew McCrea. –Maysville, MO : Blake & King, 2003

       p. ; cm.
Selected stories from the radio show "The American Countryside."

ISBN 0-9725331-0-9
       1. United States —Description and travel—Anecdotes. 2. United States—Social life and customs—Anecdotes. 3. Popular culture—United States—Anecdotes. 4. McCrea, Andrew—Journeys—United States. I. Title. II. Where does lost luggage go? III. Title: American countryside (radio program).

E169.04 .M33 2003   2002114219
973.93—dc21   0103

Cover design by Ann Pellegrino
Interior design by Debbie Sidman

Book coordination by Jenkins Group, Inc. • www.bookpublishing.com

Printed in the United States of America

06 05 04 03 02 • 5 4 3 2 1

Dedication

To my grandparents . . . whose words and lives are an example to me.

Acknowledgments

Many people have played an important part in the daily radio broadcasts and stories contained in this book. Tom Brand, Gene Millard, and the staff at KFEQ Radio first broadcast *The American Countryside* in October of 1996 and have always been extremely supportive of these features.

The Brownfield Network and Learfield Communications based in Jefferson City, Missouri, have also provided the assistance needed to gather and share the stories in this book. I also wish to thank the many radio stations who air our program and the listeners who make it possible.

To the dedicated teachers of the King City school system who provided me with a wonderful place to grow and learn. I thank you.

I also thank my parents and family for their love, support, and strength.

I thank God for the people in my life, and for the opportunity to share a few of these stories with others.

And . . . thanks to the people we meet as we "travel the countryside" who inspire the stories and teach us life's lessons along the way.

Contents

The Journey Begins
An Introduction
KING CITY, MISSOURI

> *"There's a time for departure even when
> there's no certain place to go."*
>
> — TENNESSEE WILLIAMS

Sometimes a journey begins without you realizing you are taking its first steps. It can be a path that winds through the weeks, months, and years and leads you to a place you would never have expected had you known you were beginning such a trip so long ago. This book is about journeys and the lessons each of us learn along the way. For me, the journey began in a small high school in northwest Missouri in 1989.

It was my junior year and I needed to pick up an extra English credit to satisfy entrance requirements at the University of Missouri. Since I attended a small high school (there were only twenty-four students in my class) there were not a lot of options. In fact, there was really only one option, "Creative Writing." The only problem was that the class was offered first hour, the exact same time as band.

I played the trumpet and took band every single year. I loved band. I didn't want to give that up in order to take an English class. In most schools I would have had no other choice than to drop band if I wanted to go to the university, but one of the advantages of attending a small school is the personal attention you receive. I think any single student could have gone to our principal and he would have made every effort to arrange our schedules so that we could get the classes we needed. That says a lot, and I know the students appreciated it.

I went to the high school principal with my dilemma and he worked out an arrangement for me to take band during first hour and creative writing as an "independent study" (I.S.) course. In other words, I would go to band and see the creative writing teacher at the end of each day to pick up my assignments for that class. I would be taking eight classes instead of the usual seven. This would mean extra work, but it allowed me to get both classes on my schedule.

The creative writing class' sole projects were to write the school newspaper and to produce the yearbook. The disadvantage of taking the class I.S. was that I never got to choose what topic I covered for the paper. Each Monday when story ideas were listed, everyone in class got to choose their topic. Since I was in band, I always got whatever was left on the list. Of course, it was always the absolute worst pick of the group.

Soon I found myself writing all kinds of "useless" stories that no other creative writing student would ever select. There was nothing to do but make the best of these situations. I decided that even though I was going to be writing about dull subjects, I would do everything in my power to get these stories noticed.

One spring week my topic was to write about daylight savings time. This was a story that could have been written in two sentences: "Don't forget to turn your clock forward this Saturday night. Otherwise you might be an hour late for school." On the surface, that was about all there was to say. Still, that's the topic I drew and I had to write a lot more than two sentences if I wanted a passing grade.

I began to research this topic that no one else wanted. I answered provocative questions such as, "Who began daylight savings time?" "When did it begin?" "What states do not switch their clocks?"

No, this was not journalism at its finest. It was simply my way to survive the horrid topics assigned to me. Each story I wrote seemed to be an investigative report about the mundane. What was most amazing was that people would stop me on the street to tell me they had enjoyed my article (the school paper was inserted in the local paper and went to all of the town's newspaper subscribers). They seemed to truly like these stories that I had believed no one would ever take the time to read.

Surviving creative writing class did not seem like anything special at the time. In fact, when I graduated high school in 1991, I never gave a thought to how my foray into the world of journalism might impact my life someday. It was a strange marriage of my junior year creative writing class and the National FFA (once known as the Future Farmers of America) that would begin to produce a unique career.

I had been active in the local FFA chapter from the time I was a freshman in high school. I slowly worked my way up the ranks and was fortunate to have the opportunity to serve as a state and national officer. If you are not familiar with the organization, a team of six national officers are elected each year. They take a year leave of absence from their respective universities and travel approximately 270–300 days delivering speeches, providing workshops, and visiting corporate sponsors. It was a wonderful experience for this farm boy from northwest Missouri.

When I returned to the University of Missouri to complete my last three semesters of work, I also began a broadcasting internship at the Brownfield Network, the nation's largest agricultural radio network. I completed that internship in the spring of 1996 and graduated from the university in May of that year. I returned home to the family farm, but I continued to work for the radio network in a part-time capacity.

All of these experiences created a most unique background in writing, speaking, and broadcasting. I had an interest in working with people and sharing their inspiring stories with others. The creative writing experience back in 1989 had unknowingly helped me develop a knack for finding an interesting angle to a story as well. I was still traveling to do workshops and giving speeches for a variety of groups.

Throw into this mix a young man whom I met while eating lunch at the dorm cafeteria at the university in the fall of 1991. Tom Brand was also a farm boy from northwest Missouri and the two of us stayed in occasional contact throughout college. When I heard he had landed the job as farm programming director at the local radio station, KFEQ in St. Joseph, MO, I asked if I could start my own radio feature that would highlight the people and places I encountered on my journeys. I called it "The American Countryside."

Tom and others at KFEQ agreed to give it a shot. They were more than generous in the support they provided. The Brownfield Network also agreed to take the program once I had perfected a format in St. Joseph. By 2002 the program had grown to reach almost one hundred radio stations across the Midwest, and I had begun to reformat some of the features to appear on national radio programs such as *America in the Morning* on the Westwood One radio network.

If you've never heard *The American Countryside* radio broadcasts, they are a daily three–minute feature that highlights fascinating people and places and tells their interesting stories. We bill it as a "slice of Americana." It is something similar to what radio journalist Charles Kurwalt used to produce for television.

I personally travel to interview about eighty-five percent of the people featured on the program. I will occasionally conduct an interview over the phone (this is only done when time is of the essence) and Tom Brand and others will also gather a few stories as they travel. I really don't have much of a travel budget. Almost every single interview is a result of me being in an area to speak or present a workshop at a leadership conference. I call ahead and schedule interviews at locations near where I will be. I use the phrase "in the area" very loosely. It is a relative term. For instance, on a recent trip to Raleigh, North Carolina, I determined that Washington, D.C., was "in the area" (never mind the fact that the two cities are 250 miles apart). I once flew to Columbus, Ohio, and figured that Detroit could certainly be considered "in the area" as well.

What follows are some of the experiences I have encountered while on the road gathering stories for the radio program. I traveled to each of these locations and interviewed each of the people quoted in the book, with the exception of the chapter entitled "Project Greek Island," which Tom Brand originally covered. I have not bothered to include the reason I was "in the area" unless it adds meaning to the story. Most of the time I was there because of another event a few minutes away. Sometimes you will find that I have not quoted a person in the story. That is not because they did a poor job in the interview. Each story is unique, and each story lends itself to be told in its own way.

So what is the purpose of this book? I've learned that each of the stories we put on the air often teach us a little about life. People love stories. Stories have been used for thousands of years to relate important principles of life. Jesus taught in parables. Aesop used fables. Both are ways we communicate our point in a way that is easily understandable to our audience.

I believe each of us has the ability to grow as a leader in our work, our families, and our communities. While this book won't give you reams of scientific data on leadership, it will hopefully provide some interesting and inspiring stories that will help each of us make good choices in life. You may find that some of the chapters hold a different meaning for you than they did for me. Great! That's what stories are supposed to do. They illustrate life's lessons in a context that is relevant to each of us. I hope you enjoy the features, but I also hope that, like me, you take home a lesson you might use in life.

Y ou will find that the point, or moral, of each story is included in a shaded box with a compass symbol. The first compasses were used by the Chinese almost two thousand years ago. They used lodestones, a mineral composed of iron oxide that aligns itself in a north-south direction. These natural magnets were eventually placed on squares with directional markings. Once navigators found north, they immediately knew how to find east, south, and west.

The shaded boxes in this book work much the same as a compass. These simple points are designed to give our lives direction. As we begin to apply these lessons to our lives, we will be better able to navigate the challenges we encounter every day. These boxes are part of the original story, yet they are highlighted to emphasize the "direction" they can provide us.

Although *The American Countryside* is a daily radio feature, I still live on the farm in northwest Missouri where I grew up. In fact, I am farming with my father a majority of the time (although my father seems to think I have an uncanny knack for leaving on a trip just as the weather clears enough for us to go bale hay). I also continue to speak and present programs to youth and adults from a variety of organizations. I'm on a journey that has taught me a lot about life through the lessons shared by the people and places I've met while traveling the countryside.

Over the Falls in a Barrel

Niagara Falls, New York

"In every enterprise consider where you would come out."

—Publilius Syrus

D on, a lifelong resident of Niagara Falls, was the "resident historian" of this western New York city thanks to his long tenure at the public library. Now retired from his job, I contacted him to get the scoop on a group of renegades. Don assured me that he had the entire day free to visit with me . . . except for a half hour in the evening when he and his wife had to watch *Jeopardy*. What followed was a wonderful tale over a century in the making.

The story began on October 24, 1901, when a schoolteacher named Ann Edson Taylor came to Niagara Falls. Don relayed that she and her "manager" arrived on a train from her hometown of Bay City, Michigan. She came prepared with her own four and a half foot tall barrel and a small mattress. Those tools were all she needed to attempt a feat that would make news around the world.

It was Ann's forty-sixth birthday and many wondered if it would be her last. (It *was* Ann's birthday, but exactly which birthday may never be known. It seems she often lied about how old she really was. Some say it was actually her sixty–third birthday . . . quite a variation). Ann and her crew took the barrel and stuffed the mattress inside. An anvil was placed in the bottom of the barrel to provide ballast. At that point, all that was left was for Ann to get in the barrel and tempt the forces of nature. At four o'clock in the evening, the top of the barrel was nailed shut and then lowered into the water above the falls. Soon it hit the brink of the 176-foot rapids and disappeared in the mist below.

Looking back over a century later, what happened that day was probably sheer luck. The fact that the barrel, let alone Ann, survived the plunge is remarkable considering the tremendous power of the falls. Each second, 600,000 gallons of water pour over the falls, thundering thirteen stories into the mist below. When Ann's crew fished out the barrel that day, they pried open the top and Ann emerged groggy but with only a few scratches and a bump on her head. Don added, "I think she already had a bump on her head before she got in the barrel!" Ann Edson Taylor was the first person to go over Niagara Falls in a barrel, beginning a true-to-life legend that lives today.

Only about a dozen people are documented to have gone over the falls in a barrel and survived, and the term "barrel" should be used lightly. Some of the contraptions have been far more extravagant than the simple barrel Ann used. Most people who attempt the stunt do not survive. Often they are trapped underneath the falls and the rushing waters simply pound them for minutes or hours. On some occasions, no trace of the person or barrel is ever found.

Don took out some carefully crafted index cards. He had retold the stories of the falls many times and really didn't need them. Still, he would occasionally look down at one, smile, and then begin another story. Each card triggered a new tale. In many cases, the characters he described were people he had met and knew well.

"Red Hill Jr. attempted the stunt in 1951," Don continued. "His family had boated below the falls all of his life. He knew the danger of the falls because he had seen others die attempting the stunt. In fact, he and his father had pulled many bodies from the river, dead or alive. Still, Hill Jr. was convinced he could attempt the stunt and add his name to the list of successful thrill seekers. He probably felt pressure to live up to the legend of his father, who had accomplished many stunts and saved many lives around the falls.

"Red Hill Jr. spent the summer of 1951 perfecting a contraption he dubbed 'The Thing.' He constructed a craft consisting of thirteen large heavy duty inner tubes, lashed together with canvass and heavy fish netting. Hill went over the falls on the afternoon of August 5, but "The Thing" was caught under the powerful falls and broken into many pieces."

Don concluded, "It just wasn't it. Red Hill perished at the falls, just as he had witnessed many others die."

On July 9, 1960, a boy named Roger became the first person to go over the falls *without* a barrel and survive. He was seven years old. He was in a boat with two others when the motor failed and the craft began to drift toward the falls, eventually capsizing just above the brink. Roger, buoyed by a mere life jacket, floated over the torrent and survived. One person drowned; the other was pulled to shore before going over the falls. "And Roger still lives today," said Don, as he completed another story and moved on to his next card.

Fines can range to $10,000 or more if you try the stunt (and live to be able to pay up). The worst part, Don pointed out, is the fact that so many rescue workers' lives are put at risk when they are called upon to save a daredevil at the base of the falls.

Don reminded me to tell people to come and enjoy the falls, to come and have their honeymoons there. But, he admonished, do not come to western New York to take a ride over the falls. He already has enough of those index cards.

Ironically, I doubt that many of us had ever heard of Ann Edson Taylor before reading this story. Most of us have heard of people going over the falls in a barrel, but almost no one can tell you the name of anyone who did. Why aren't these individuals remembered? After all, didn't they risk their lives in pursuit of their goals?

We pay tribute to those who risk their lives, or even lose their lives, in pursuit of a "worthy" goal. Not all heroes have giant memorials built in their honor, but we usually honor and remember people for what they do for others. We pay tribute to how they helped society or bettered the lives of those around them.

The daredevils who survived their ride in a barrel took such a risk for their own glory. (In fact, Ann Edson Taylor "passed the hat" after her success in order to reap a monetary gain, though Don said she never became wealthy nor did she ever become a household name). True leaders believe in causes that reach far beyond their own welfare. They work to improve the lives of others and to build communities.

The Studebakers

SOUTH BEND, INDIANA

"When you're through changing, you're through."

—BRUCE BARTON

Today these old assembly buildings sit vacant in northern Indiana, a silent memorial to a car company that revolutionized the transportation industry. This city is known for Notre Dame University, but once it was also known as one of the most prominent automobile manufacturing centers in the U.S. It's an interesting story of how companies can use "change" as a springboard to success or ignore it and plunge into failure.

Two brothers. Sixty-eight dollars. One blacksmith shop. That's how things began in February 1852 in South Bend, Indiana, when Henry and Clement Studebaker opened their business and began building wagons.

In 1858, another brother would change the way that small shop would operate. John Studebaker moved back from California and bought out his brother Henry. John had made a small fortune on the west coast during the gold rush. He never struck gold, but he struck it rich by selling wheelbarrows to miners.

John provided the money to expand the business; the Civil War provided the reason to expand it. Another local wagon manufacturer had a contract to build one hundred wagons in seventy-two hours for the Union army. When the company holding that contract couldn't fill it, the Studebakers stepped in and built the needed wagons. Their business flourished.

By the end of the nineteenth century, the Studebaker Brothers Manufacturing Company was the world's largest maker of horse-drawn vehicles. With the advent of the "horseless" carriage at the end of that same century, you might have thought that the Studebaker's success would be short lived. After all, the need for wagons would soon be gone.

The transformation the Studebakers were able to make is remarkable. They were the world's largest wagon makers, yet they saw change coming and took steps to keep their business from vanishing. In 1897 they built an experimental automobile and by 1904 Studebaker offered its first gasoline powered vehicles. During the first two decades of the twentieth century, Studebaker would sell both wagons and automobiles side-by-side. Not only were the Studebakers taking advantage of a new market, they were still reaping the benefits of their original business. Finally, in 1920, with wagon sales continuing to decline, Studebaker sold its wagon business and focused on auto production.

On February 15, 1952, the Studebaker Company concluded its first century in business. Vehicle number 7,130,874 rolled out of the South Bend factory on that day. It was outstanding foresight that helped the car manufacturer make the successful transition from wagons to cars in the early twentieth century. It was a lack of foresight that would spell the company's demise in the 1960s.

In many ways, the Studebaker Company did not heed the lessons learned in its early days. By the 1950s and '60s, the company was building cars in antiquated facilities. Soon, Studebaker was lagging far behind its competitors. In December of 1963, production ceased in South Bend. By the end of the decade, Studebaker ceased manufacturing vehicles of any kind.

The Studebaker story makes it clear that while leaders cannot always predict the future, great leaders see the importance of always looking to the future. They develop a sense of foresight and a willingness to embrace new facets of an industry. This is not change for the sake of change. It is change for the sake of survival. It is not a blind leap, but a jump based on sound beliefs about coming trends. Studebaker will long be remembered for an amazing transition from the world's largest wagon maker to a large and respected auto maker. The company will also be remembered for a lack of foresight that would lead to the closing of the company.

The Flying Wallendas

SEDALIA, MISSOURI

"Men of genius are admired,
men of wealth are envied,
men of power are feared;
but only men of character are trusted."

—UNKNOWN

Tino Wallenda was only seven years old when his grandfather, Karl, put him on a tightrope. From that day on, Tino would continue a family tradition that dates to the 1700s. For well over two centuries the Wallendas have been wowing circus crowds. Their work on the flying trapeze and tightrope has earned them the nickname "The Flying Wallendas."

When I caught up with the Wallendas, they were performing daily shows at the Missouri State Fair. We sat down next to the tightrope towers and began to visit about their exciting and very dangerous career. Tino told me that most of the time he and his family walk ropes that are about thirty feet in the air. They never work with a safety net. That means it really doesn't matter how far above the ground the rope is set. A fall from any height almost always has the same end . . . death.

Working without a net, of course, makes you a better tightrope walker. Tino says, "Strangely enough, that is a safety factor. Because we don't have a net we really work on our routines. Without a net you might say, 'Well it's windy but we've got a safety valve right there and nothing can happen.' Friends of mine have lost their lives because of a net when they bounced out and were killed."

Some people believe Tino uses magic instead of skill. "It's funny what people think. Some people believe we have mirrors up there and that it's really a plank we walk. They sometimes ask me about the magnets in my shoes. Someone once told me they knew why we used those balancing poles. If you fall you stick the pole in the ground and pole vault to safety!"

But Tino doesn't use magic. He performs a very real routine on a wire about five-eighths of an inch wide. This career can have very real consequences. In 1962, while performing their famous seven-person pyramid, one of the members lost his balance. Three men fell to the ground. Two were killed. The third man, Tino's uncle, was paralyzed from the waist down. In 1978, Tino's grandfather, the man who first put young Tino on the tightrope, attempted a crossing between two buildings in Puerto Rico. An equipment problem caused Karl Wallenda to fall to his death.

Tino has walked on wires above dens of lions, across rivers, and even over a pool of fifty "man-eating" sharks. He says the most important thing his grandfather taught him was to focus his attention on a point at the other end of the wire that was unmoving. That is how he maintains his balance. Tino has carried each of his children across the highwire. He says they were never scared. They simply had trust in their daddy to carry them safely across the span.

Each of us knows what it is like to have someone we can trust. It is a comforting feeling. If trust is ever lost, it is often very difficult to find again. That's why trust is such a powerful and precious commodity for leaders. It is the very foundation of leadership. Such leaders focus on character . . . a constant and unwavering set of values by which they lead their lives. Their focus on these values builds a sense of trust with those around them.

Tino uses his work as an opportunity to speak to religious gatherings and revivals too. It takes the issue of trust to a spiritual level. He asks people to think about whom they can trust, even after death. The question is an introduction to the topic of faith. Tino explains to groups that, ultimately, his faith and trust is in Christ. It's a story that has been shared with Tino's audiences around the world and has even appeared in print in magazines such as *Decision*, a publication of the Billy Graham Evangelistic Association.

Just like Tino, there is not a safety net for those who betray trust. You cannot hop up again without serious consequences. Would others trust you to "carry" them just like Tino carried his children across the tightrope? Do you have a constant set of values and beliefs that guide your life? Do your words and actions exemplify trust? For the Wallendas, trust is what keeps them flying high above the crowd, continuing to fascinate audiences for seven generations.

Where Does Lost Luggage Go?

SCOTTSBORO, ALABAMA

"The tragedy of life is what dies inside a man while he lives."

—ALBERT SCHWEITZER

It's inevitable. If you spend enough time flying, there will come a time when you and your luggage will not arrive at your destination at the same time. If you're lucky, the airlines can track down that wayward bag and get it back to you quickly. But every year thousands of bags cannot be reunited with their owners. Where do they go? Many are trucked here, to this town of fifteen thousand tucked in the hills of Appalachia, halfway between Birmingham and Chattanooga.

It's been called "the final resting place" for lost luggage. Begun by the Owens family in 1970, the Unclaimed Baggage Center (UBC) purchases "lost" luggage and cargo from the airlines. Air carriers will spend ninety days working to reunite such property with its owners. After that, the merchandise is sold to UBC.

UBC buys the luggage without knowing its contents. It's like Christmas every day, with employees opening luggage and sorting through what's inside. The best items are cleaned and refurbished and sold at UBC's retail store while other items may be donated to charity or simply thrown away. With so much luggage arriving in Scottsboro, the UBC is able to offer about seven thousand new items in its store every day. The UBC looks just like most retail stores, with departments for clothing, electronics, sports, and camping equipment. The difference is that all of the merchandise for sale once belonged to an airline passenger (the UBC also deals with lost cargo, but much of the merchandise did once belong to passengers themselves).

Most of the items "discovered" when bags are opened are just ordinary clothes and travel gear. But, occasionally, it is like finding hidden treasure. One day a worn old bag showed up at UBC. Upon opening the suitcase, the items inside were deemed worthy of a trash bin. As the UBC employees searched though, they noticed some dirty rags wrapped up in the bottom of the suitcase. Inside those rags was a 5.8-carat diamond ring!

There is even a museum inside the store devoted to the unusual and precious items recovered. Some memorable finds include a violin and bagpipes, a Stetson hat autographed by Muhammad Ali, and a camera used aboard the space shuttle. Yet another suitcase yielded some interesting looking electronic equipment. After an expert examined the device, it was found to be the guidance system for an F16! UBC immediately contacted the Air Force to see if they could help piece together the unusual story. The military was very glad to get the call. They had believed the guidance system had fallen into the hands of the Iranians. Instead, it was sitting at UBC in Scottsboro, Alabama.

One gentleman drove up from Atlanta to buy a pair of ski boots for his wife. When he arrived back home, she tried on the boots to see if they would fit. The boots felt great. She just happened to pull back the tongue of one boot to discover her maiden name. They were her boots. She had lost them two years earlier before she was married (in such unusual cases, the items still must be purchased since the airline already compensated the passenger for the lost luggage).

There is even a selection of wedding dresses at the store. Hopefully they were not lost just before the ceremonies they were intended for! It is truly amazing to see the wide array of items that couldn't find their way home. Those items usually end up here because they were not labeled. But how can a person lose a wedding dress, a camera used on the space shuttle, or God forbid, the guidance system to an F16? Aren't these items so valuable that their owners would take extra care to label and protect them? If they were lost, wouldn't they take every step possible to locate them?

One of the most important things we human beings can do is take an inventory of what is important in our lives. Do we spend time with those who are important to us? Do we tell them how much they mean to us? Our own health and welfare are important, yet many times we abuse our bodies through poor diets or a lack of exercise. We may say that our faith is important to us, yet we spend very little time strengthening it.

So . . . what is most precious in your life? What have you done to protect and preserve your precious "luggage?" Visitors to the UBC may shake their heads in disbelief at the items that have arrived here. Don't leave behind the most precious items in your life.

War of the Worlds

GROVER'S MILL, NEW JERSEY

"Trust everybody, but cut the cards."

—FINLEY PETER DUNNE

Today the town of Grover's Mill, New Jersey, does not exist on most road maps. It has long since been swallowed by the suburbs of Princeton. But on October 30, 1938, just about everyone across the nation knew exactly where the little town was located. Most thought it had been removed from the maps that night.

It was a hot summer afternoon when Lolly Dey and I saw down in our lawn chairs in the small park near her home. As we found a spot under a large shade tree, we talked about how this area was once surrounded by farmsteads when she was a little girl. For the most part, the events here at Grover's Mill have been, well, uneventful. But what supposedly transpired here October 30, 1938, still brings visitors to see the spot where humanity was to face its most formidable opponent.

Lolly was a young girl back in 1938. It was a Sunday night as she headed to evening church services where she played the piano for the small weekly gathering. However, just a few minutes into that service, the peaceful hymn singing would come to a sudden and shocking close.

A stranger barged through the church door, exclaiming, "The Martians have landed at Grover's Mill!" The news was all over the radio, he exclaimed. The invaders were here and everyone should run to defend their families and their town.

The crowd was shocked, of course. The message was certainly strange, but Lolly believed the man. The fact that the news was on the radio seemed to give the story credibility. Actually, she thought the "Martians" might be someone else. She recalled her history teacher discussing Hitler's growing army in Europe. Lolly thought the Martians were actually the Germans invading the nation.

The pastor suggested that everyone bow their heads for prayer. Lolly also said her own prayer and asked God to please spare the world. The congregation was obviously worried and many still had family at home, so the pastor dismissed the group to go and protect their loved ones.

Of the millions of Americans who were home that evening, many had tuned into their favorite programs on the radio. Orson Welles' broadcast was on the air, a program that often featured plays directed by Welles himself. His one-hour radio program that night was a dramatization of H. G. Wells' *War of the Worlds*. Although the beginning of the program clearly stated that the night's feature would be a dramatization, those who tuned in late missed that all-important message.

News bulletins stated that a flaming object of unknown origin had landed on a farmstead near Grover's Mill. Soon, reporters on the scene described alien creatures that had emerged from a spacecraft and used flame to kill several onlookers. The broadcast continued to keep listeners on the edges of their seats as one actor, playing the part of a news reporter, stated, "Incredible as it may seem, both the observations of science and the evidence of our eyes leads to the inescapable assumption that those strange beings who landed in the New Jersey farmlands tonight are the vanguard of an invading army from the planet Mars."

It is reported that one resident of Grover's Mill even shot at the watertower, believing it to be one of the invading spacecraft. Other residents fled the area, fearing for their lives. There is a story that one area family gathered everyone together, hopped in the car, and drove into Pennsylvania before learning the broadcasts were a hoax. In their hurry, the husband "accidentally" left his mother behind.

When Lolly hurried home from church, her mother couldn't imagine why she was back so early. All of Lolly's fears were soon put to rest when her mother, who had heard the opening of the program, assured her that there was no reason to be worried. Still, thousands of Americans scrambled to safety and jammed phone lines to local police stations.

Lolly and I sat just a few feet from a marker that had been placed in Van Nest Park commemorating the site as the fictitious landing spot of Martians that October evening. I asked Lolly if she was mad at Welles because of the furor he had caused. She said she wasn't. "I just thanked God that this wasn't the end of the world," she explained. Others weren't as forgiving as Lolly. No one knows for sure if Welles intended to manufacture such a national panic. Even if he did, he probably never imagined the magnitude of the scare he would create.

The broadcast captured national media attention everywhere. Dorothy Thompson of the *New York Tribune* wrote of the Welles drama, "Mr. Orson Welles and the Mercury Theater of the Air have made one of the most fascinating and important demonstrations of all time. They have proved that a few effective voices, accompanied by sound effects, can convince masses of people of a totally unreasonable, completely fantastic proposition as to create a nation-wide panic."

She continued, "Hitler managed to scare all of Europe to its knees a month ago, but he at least had an army and an air force to back up his shrieking words. But Mr. Welles scared thousands into demoralization with nothing at all."

Certainly no one can blame Lolly and others for their reactions to the events of that evening. However, the *War of the Worlds* broadcast taught the entire nation that you can't always believe everything you hear. In some cases, the best course of action is to stop and check your sources. As the old saying goes, "Some people just like to blow a lot of smoke." We just have to make sure there is an actual fire. Otherwise, our worst fears may be nothing more than fiction.

"Let him who would move the world, first move himself."

—SOCRATES

I was already in my window seat reading the newspaper. I knew the flight to L.A. would be full, so I made an occasional glance toward the front of the plane to scan the passengers. I wondered who might be sitting next to me.

Soon a group of young men began to make their way down the aisle. I kept an eye on them; they looked much different from most passengers I see. As they moved closer I could tell that each of them had enough tattoos and body piercings to keep a body art parlor in business for at least a couple of years. Their wardrobe was a cross between biker garb and clothing you would find at a second-hand store. These were definitely some tough hombres and I wondered why they might be headed to L.A. I just hoped the security screeners had done their job before letting them into the terminal.

In all the flights I had made, I had never seen any passenger who looked quite like this. Of course, you can imagine exactly where they were heading. Soon five of them had settled into the two seats next to me and the three seats across the aisle. There were six people in their group and, frankly, it was the sixth member of the group who scared me. He boarded the plane a few minutes after the other five.

He was wearing similar garb to the others, with plenty of tattoos and piercings. One other thing stood out about this young man. He had a very long red beard that he had braided into a ponytail that hung from his chin to his waist. The long braided beard swung back and forth as he headed down the aisle of the plane.

He came to our row and looked at the other members of his party. He angrily stated, "They did it to us again, didn't they? They didn't get the six of us seats together!"

I could feel his stare blazing right through the paper I was pretending to read. Actually, the airline had gotten five of them seats together, but this sixth man was out of luck. I had the fortune to be sitting in that sixth seat. I crouched further behind my paper, sinking into seat 16F as if I hadn't heard what he said. When I had seen him walking down the aisle, he'd looked like he might be a pro wrestler. I was making plans for a quick escape from the plane.

A flight attendant got his attention and took him toward the front of the plane. She assured him that she had a great seat along the aisle in the front. This seemed to satisfy him. The other five quickly fell asleep.

I treated my five companions as if they were sleeping babies. I did not want to disturb them. They never spoke to me and I never made an effort to say anything to them. I imagined that anything I had to say might give them cause to riot.

Halfway through our flight to L.A. a young woman came up to our row. She stopped and tapped one of the men on the shoulder. I shuddered. What could she want? Hadn't she heard the adage, "Let sleeping dogs lie"? There was sure to be a brawl now and I was confident they would go after the guy who was sitting in their sixth seat.

The man roused from his sleep and his eyes attempted to focus on the person who had just awakened him.

"I'm so sorry to bother you, but I wondered if I could get your autograph?" she asked.

Autograph? From these hooligans? Why? Didn't she see what they were wearing? They were obviously headed to a gang summit.

He signed his name, thanked the young lady, and went back to sleep.

Who were these guys? I wasn't about to wake them and ask them. That would be kind of embarrassing. I began to study them more closely, like a detective looking for clues to solve his case. The only identification I could find was a strange logo that appeared to be on all their carry-on bags. It was a yellow logo with the letters "Lit" emblazoned in blue.

We landed in L.A. and pulled up to the gate. The five began to stir to life and collect the items they had brought on board. What should I do? Should I actually ask them their identity?

Before I could answer my own question, another young lady appeared at our aisle. "My brother and I really enjoy your music. We were at one of your last concerts. Could I get your autograph?"

By now passengers were making their way off the plane. Having signed another autograph, the five headed down the aisle, out the jet way, and disappeared in the mass of passengers inside the terminal.

As soon as I got to a shopping mall I headed to a music store. I began to look at music in the rock/alternative section. I finally came to a cd labeled "Lit." I flipped over the cd and there they were. The pictures of the young men who had ridden next to me on the plane were on the back of that cd.

This wasn't any random band. In the summer of 1999, Lit's hit "My Own Worst Enemy" was one of the most played songs on the radio, rocketing its way up the music charts. I had passed up my chance to visit with a celebrity rock band!

ince then, I've always made an effort to speak to others and learn more about them. We don't have to adopt the style and beliefs of everyone we meet, but it is important to understand others. Too often we label people as "different" and we consequently pass up opportunities. If we hope to make a positive difference in the world around us, we can't just choose to pass people by who aren't like us. You never know, you just might meet a superstar.

VLA

SOCORRO, NEW MEXICO

*"You can't depend on your eyes when
your imagination is out of focus."*

—SAMUEL CLEMENS (MARK TWAIN)

Sixty miles east of Socorro, New Mexico, in a barren stretch of land called the "Plains of San Agustin," twenty-seven "eyes" peer deep into space. They are twenty-seven radio telescope antennas that make up the Very Large Array (VLA), the largest radio telescope in the world. Together, they demonstrate the power we have to peer into the deepest reaches of space.

Radio astronomy is a science very difficult to explain. We might think of "radio waves" as something we hear, but that isn't necessarily the case. In fact, radio waves are just one type of waves, such as gamma rays and X-rays, which are around us all the time. Radio waves cannot be seen by the human eye; however, radio astronomers can use antennas to "see" the radio waves emitted by an object in space. That data is then turned into a picture of the gases and particles moving through space. In other words, radio waves are turned into a picture of an object in space.

Radio astronomy allows us to see things that optical telescopes cannot detect. For instance, the VLA has allowed us to research jets of subatomic particles streaming from the centers of black holes. The VLA has been used by more astronomers and has produced more scientific papers than any other radio telescope in the world. Only the Hubble Space Telescope can give us a deeper look into space, and it of course is not based on Earth but circles the planet in outer space.

The beauty of the VLA is that it is composed of twenty-seven separate dishes that can be moved to different positions. The antennas are placed along a set of railroad tracks arranged in a "Y" pattern. A specialized diesel engine is used to move the dishes about every four months. The tracks extend up to thirteen miles from the center. This gives the VLA the resolution of an antenna twenty-two miles across with the sensitivity of a dish 422 feet in diameter.

If you've seen the movie *Contact* you've seen the VLA. In that movie, Jodie Foster plays the role of a scientist attempting to make contact with extraterrestrials. In real life the VLA is not used to listen for "aliens," although researchers say the movie did increase public awareness of the important contributions astronomy makes in our world.

As I stood next to one of the eighty-two-foot-wide dishes, I heard its gears gently begin to turn. Just as a flower tilts upward to follow the path of the sun, the large dish slowly rotated upward until it pointed straight into the sky. I stood back to watch as each of these 230-ton behemoths began to move together, a quiet ballet of radio antennas waltzing among cattle grazing on the surrounding plains. It was a beautiful sight to see.

Whether you are an astronomer or not, the VLA has affected our everyday lives. For example, doctors used to routinely perform exploratory surgery on patients. Thanks to the principles used in radio astronomy, technology such as CAT scans and MRI, are now possible. These methods don't take a look into space but instead look inside our own bodies.

Standing here on the Plains of San Augustin, you realize the power of focus . . . twenty-seven dishes, peering up to thirteen billion light years into space, reading radio waves that are translated into pictures we can see. No other place on Earth can see farther from "home" than right here at the VLA. A shared focus helps us to see what was once out of reach. Each of us begins to create that picture when we take a look at what we hope to achieve in our future. With such a focus, our distant dreams can become realities, creating a wonderful picture of life never before seen.

"A man who does not plan long ahead
will find trouble right at his door."

—Confucius

W hen family members can't get together for Thanksgiving, they often give one another a phone call. Parents and grandparents, aunts and uncles, brothers and sisters—they each make calls to one another to exchange news over the holiday. They may end up placing dozens of calls and talking for many hours.

But each Thanksgiving, Sherleen Clausen's "family" receives about eight thousand phone calls. Her adopted family of home economists takes calls in the Chicago suburb of Downer's Grove at Butterball's turkey talk-line. Every Thanksgiving, Sherleen leaves her own family to work a shift at the call center. Although the talk-line fields questions nearly year-round, the highest volume call day is, of course, Thanksgiving.

To see this room on most days, you will simply find a large conference room with a few tables and chairs scattered about for impromptu meetings. But as Thanksgiving approaches, this area is transformed into a nerve center to field the calls of distressed cooks coast to coast. In the months of November and December alone, the staff of home economists will field over 100,000 calls.

Most of the folks who call Sherleen on Thanksgiving are turkeys in trouble. When I say "turkeys in trouble" I am referring to the cooks, not the birds. The home economists say it's amazing how many people call on Thanksgiving to report that their ovens don't work, as if this was somehow the General Electric repair line. In fact, one man once called to say that the wires on the back of his stove were smoking. They told him to hang up and dial 9-1-1.

Besides ovens that don't work, it seems many people have trouble thawing their turkeys. The usual problem is that they don't begin early enough. With the Thanksgiving feast approaching, the cooks turn to desperate measures to quickly thaw the bird. It is baffling to hear of the desperate extremes cooks will resort to when the meal is on the line. One gentleman even called to say he had resorted to thawing his turkey by using his hair dryer.

On another occasion, a family's children hijacked a seventeen-pound bird and decided to take a bubble bath with it! The talk-line successfully walked the family through the steps needed to still cook the bird. The bird was eaten for Thanksgiving dinner . . . making the guests, not the cooks, the true turkeys.

Sherleen explains, "We're a team, we're all working together and sometimes you might get a question that does momentarily stump you." However, by consulting with other chefs fielding calls, the Butterball staffers can usually put their minds together and come up with an answer to almost any problem. Still, it's amazing the breadth of calls the talk-line will receive.

Sherleen remembers visiting with a lady in New York who found that her oven wasn't big enough to hold the giant bird she had purchased. "She was trying to cook the turkey but she couldn't get the door closed because the pan was too big. She wanted to go the Macy's Thanksgiving Day parade and she was wondering if she stuffed foil in the crack of the oven door whether she could hold the heat well enough and still go off and watch the parade." Sherleen agreed that it might work, but Butterball really had not done any research on baking turkeys in half open ovens.

"Another call I remember was from people traveling across the country in a motor home. They were wondering if they drove faster whether the turkey would cook faster in their mobile home." Sherleen explained that the physics of preparing the bird would not be any different no matter how fast they decided to cruise down the highway.

Then there was the infamous case involving a curious Chihuahua. The poor pooch was just too inquisitive while the chef was not watching the meal. When the cook returned, she found that the dog's head was stuck in the open cavity of the turkey. Thankfully the dog was rescued from the squeeze. No word on whether the family decided to eat the bird.

It's not all bad, though. Some chefs call in to share their great culinary ideas. A few years ago a man called to say he had found a wonderful way to baste his turkey. He began cooking the turkey and then removed the bird to use the juice produced during the first portion of cooking. He soaked a piece of cloth in the juice and placed it over the turkey for the rest of the baking process. The cloth gave the turkey a great, savory taste. It sounded like a wonderful idea until he disclosed that the cloth he was using was one of his baby's diapers!

Fortunately, most calls do turn out well. Tragedies are averted, meals are rescued, and guests go home with full stomachs. The turkey talk-line does remind us of some important lessons that reach far beyond putting the turkey in the oven. When taking on a task that is a little above your head, begin early and ask for advice. Too many novice cooks call two hours before the dinner and still have a frozen bird. You just can't thaw a turkey that quickly.

How many problems we would avoid in our own lives if we would simply ask for timely advice *and* if we would begin the task with plenty of time. Beginning early allows for the mistakes we may make. So, put away your hair dryers, rescue the turkey from the kid's bathtub, and keep the diaper on the baby. Don't be a turkey—ask for advice and plan ahead.

The Seeing Eye

MORRISTOWN, NEW JERSEY

"He who knows only his own side of the case,
knows little of that."

—JOHN STUART MILL

I n Morristown, New Jersey, it isn't uncommon to see men and women walking the streets with blindfolds covering their eyes. It's all part of the training at a remarkable institute that began in 1929. It's called The Seeing Eye and is an organization devoted to training guide dogs for the blind. In fact, only dogs trained here in Morristown may legally be called "Seeing Eye" dogs. All other dogs are simply called guide dogs.

The history of The Seeing Eye can be traced to the work of Dorothy Harrison Eustis, an American living in Switzerland. She became acquainted with a program in Pottsdam, Germany, that was training German shepherds to guide blinded veterans of World War I. Eustis wrote about the rewarding work in an article for the *Saturday Evening Post* in November of 1927.

A young blind man living in Nashville, Tennessee, Morris Frank, heard about the article and wrote to Eustis asking her to train a dog for him. He in turn would work to establish a school in the U.S. to train more dogs for blind people. When Frank made the trip to Switzerland, the ship's crew labeled him as baggage. They did not know how to handle a blind person on ship. The experience just went to show how difficult transportation and everyday life could be for blind people at the time.

Frank's first dog, Buddy, became the first guide dog in America. Eustis and Frank established The Seeing Eye in 1929. The name came from the title of Eustis' article for the *Post*. That phrase also can be found in Proverbs 20:12: "The seeing eye, the hearing ear; the Lord hath made them both." The school was moved to Morristown two years later to move closer to prominent dog breeders and to take advantage of a better training climate.

Peter Lang, in charge of training at The Seeing Eye, explained the process that is used to train the canine guides. When the pups reach seven weeks of age, they are placed in the homes of volunteer puppy-raisers. There they are taught basic obedience and good manners, while being exposed to a variety of social situations, until they are eighteen months old. At that point, the dogs head back to The Seeing Eye for their formal training, which lasts about four months.

The dogs are first trained on quiet residential streets in Morristown. Gradually the program allows dogs to encounter busier streets. Halfway through the four-month training period, trainers test their dogs while wearing blindfolds to simulate the experience of a dog guiding a blind person (a "sighted" instructor is also present for safety). A final blindfold test is administered at the end of the training period to ensure the dog is ready to be placed with a blind person.

I asked Lang what the most difficult part of training these dogs was. I figured that the most difficult part would be to cross a busy city street. Dogs are color-blind, so they can't see the color of stoplights. When the dog's owner hears traffic moving in a direction parallel to the direction he want to go, he will give the command "forward." At that point the dog must decide if the street is actually safe to cross. The guide may decide to disobey the command based on what the dog sees, perhaps a car making a right on red. This is called "intelligent disobedience." While this is a very important part of the dogs training, Lang says the dogs learn the skill quickly since they too want to avoid being hit by a car.

"So what is the most difficult part of the training?" I asked. Lang smiled and simply replied, "Tree limbs."

What he meant was that any overhead obstacle that can be a danger to a person who cannot see. A tree limb five feet high will not strike a dog, but it will smack a blind person in the face. It takes time to teach a dog to put itself in the place of the blind person. The dog must realize it is no longer "just" a dog. It is attached to a human, and the two must function as one. Over time, the dog learns to look at life with a different perspective. The canine's eyes truly must view the world from the human's point-of-view too.

After four months of training, dogs graduate from the program. The breeding, training and care of a Seeing Eye dog costs the institute about $50,000 per dog. A blind person pays only $150 for a dog, the same rate that was charged in 1934. Donations to The Seeing Eye make up the rest of the cost.

As leaders we have to learn to look at life through the eyes of those around us. What is commonplace to us may be new or uncomfortable to others. A Seeing Eye dog learns that it is not only caring for itself, it is caring for the person holding on to its harness. Do we care for others in the same way? The relationship between a Seeing Eye dog and its master depends on the dog looking at life with a new perspective. Learning lessons from The Seeing Eye can help us gain a new perspective on life as well.

Complaint Man

ATLANTA, GEORGIA

*"Great discoveries and improvements invariably
involve the cooperation of many minds."*

—ALEXANDER GRAHAM BELL

Richard has every reason to hate his job. Almost every single day, all day long, people come to him with their complaints. Yet, to Richard, this position is one that brings him some of the biggest thrills and biggest smiles in life.

Richard is a complaint resolution agent at Atlanta's Hartsfield International Airport. In other words, Richard is a troubleshooter. Each day at the world's busiest airport he has to handle a myriad of new problems and solutions. Some of the "easier" situations to resolve are missed flight connections or helping a family get seats together on a plane. But after working these gates for twenty-three years, Richard has had to deal with much more difficult problems than these.

"In my job you either love people or hate yourself, because you can really take a beating," he explained. Richard's mortal enemy is the weather . . . not just the weather in Atlanta but weather around the world. Some city in the world is almost certain to have weather problems. That means flights from those points will be delayed or canceled. When the end of the day comes, Richard may find himself getting hotel rooms for stranded passengers. The airlines will often book several hundred hotel rooms each night just to accommodate such passengers.

Sometimes there are life and death situations. The control tower may call Richard to let him know a flight is on the way with an ill passenger on board. He is often the first person to get to the plane as it pulls up to the gate. An ambulance crew is usually right behind him to assess the situation.

It may sound strange, but Richard finds his job exhilarating. He finds it a thrill to turn negatives into positives, and he has some fascinating stories to tell. For example, over the years Richard has come to know two ladies who are huge fans of country singer Kenny Rogers. They follow him around the nation and have logged over 100,000 miles just to see the singer perform at almost every one of his stops. They carry a dozen roses with them wherever they go, so they can hand deliver them to the famous entertainer.

One day their plane arrived late in Atlanta. The pair had to get to Las Vegas that evening in time to deliver their usual dozen roses to Rogers. Richard worked hard to find them a new route and, after a lot of effort, ended up getting them there on time. Over a year later, the pair, roses in hand, spotted Richard in Atlanta and ran up to him and gave him a big hug for saving the day. It's just one of the "perks" of the job.

On another day, a flight was oversold and it was up to Richard to re-ticket several passengers. Spirits were low and some people had directed their anger toward Richard. He decided to turn the gate house into a game show. Instead of *The Price Is Right* Richard called the show the *The Flight Is Right*. When it was time for a passenger to get his or her new ticket, he would call out the individual's name and shout, "Come on down, you're the next contestant on *The Flight Is Right!*" One young mother's name was called and her toddler in a diaper followed along behind her. The pair were quite excited and the mother picked up the child and placed her on the ticket counter. As the passengers gave a round of applause, the child's diaper fell off. Richard says it was the most memorable moment he has had in his twenty-three years.

"**W**e try to empathize and put ourselves in the customer's shoes. I handle the customer just like I would want to be treated," he said. It's very good advice for each of us, no matter what job we do. Richard hopes people realize, "In life we always have things that are going to go wrong no matter what we do." You can't expect good fortune every minute of every day. When tough problems arise, stay calm, be patient, and begin looking for solutions. It's the approach Richard uses every day to handle problems at the world's busiest airport.

Talk Show Host

JEFFERSON CITY, MISSOURI

> "A sensible man never embarks on an enterprise
> until he can see his way clear to the end of it."
>
> —AESOP

I t was my first day as a talk show host. Since I am in the radio business, I had been around talk shows for many years and I thought I knew quite a bit about how such shows worked. Still, I was nervous about my first solo appearance as a guest host for the talk show that originated from the Brownfield Network studios. Could I ask intelligent questions of my guests? Could I handle the callers? I was excited and apprehensive all at the same time.

I had lined up a great guest for my inaugural show. He was a young entrepreneur who had created a space tourism business and he planned to offer trips into outer space within a few years. In fact, 150 people had already paid several hundred dollars to "hold" their place in line, to get one of the first tickets into outer space.

I read over notes about the business. I read magazine articles about the space tourism industry. I knew the topic would generate plenty of interest from many listeners, and I was ready to discuss the subject with knowledge to spare.

It was four minutes past the top of the hour. Two more minutes and the theme music would begin to play. At that moment, the producer, sitting just across the glass from me, gave me an important message via my headset. No one at the space tourism business knew where the president was. He had disappeared. Until they could locate him, I was on my own.

So there I was. I had the perfect topic, but no guest. I don't really know what I said during the first ten-minute segment of the show. I recited every fact I knew about the solar system. I muttered useless facts about planets like Neptune and Pluto. I read from the press releases and magazine articles I had researched. All the while, the producer stayed on the line as an entire company searched for their president.

The good news was I had filled the first ten minutes. The bad news was, I had used up every piece of material I had and I still had another forty-four minutes to fill!

When they finally found the absent-minded president, he was kind enough to come on the air and fill six whole minutes before he jetted off to another meeting. That was it. The interview I had set up weeks ahead of time, the interview that was to last an entire hour, lasted six minutes.

Now was the time when I would see if I had what it took to be a talk show host. I asked my audience questions. Were any of them still listening? Would any of them call in to save me? I rambled on, looking at my computer screen, hoping the blinking cursor would soon change to a caller's name.

Almost all talk shows use a call screener. The host is then able to look at a computer screen and see the caller's name, city, or state, and the topic they wish to discuss. I could handle up to five calls at one time. At this moment, I would settle for just one.

Finally, I could see the producer frantically typing me a message. There it was. "Billy" from Missouri was on the line. I didn't wait long enough to see what he wished to discuss. I was already stating that we were headed to line number four (as if line numbers one through three were already filled) to talk to Billy in Missouri.

Billy sounded as if he had just come out of hibernation. His slow drawl and crude English didn't make him the most articulate caller I could have received.

He said, "Ya know where I'd like ta go if I was gonna take a trip in ta outa space?"

Did I really want to know? Did anybody want to know? Billy was all I had. I was still staring at approximately thirty-four minutes to fill. So I gladly said, "Where do you want to go, Billy?"

Billy said, "If I got ta go anywhere I could want ta go in the una verse, I'd think I'd go to Utopia. Ya know where Utopia is?"

Utopia. I had always been told that Utopia was a fictional place, an imaginary state of well being. There was no exact place called "Utopia." It was wherever a person wanted it to be.

At this point I began to concentrate on the red "kill" button next to my monitor. What was "utopia" to Billy? Could his definition really go out over the airwaves? The way Billy sounded, I thought he was already in a state of Utopia. In fact, he might be smoking something right now that was sending him to Utopia.

I inched my hand closer to the button that would drop Billy from the airwaves (the talk show operated on a delay. Anything Billy said was delayed three seconds before it went out over the air).

Billy demanded, "Do ya know where Utopia is?"

I stammered, "I don't think I know."

Suddenly it seemed that Billy came out of his slow drawl. Intelligence suddenly seemed to enter his brain and shed light on his words. The southern Missouri hillbilly was about to change into a great man of science.

"Utopia is one of Jupiter's moons." (That's not exactly true. "Europa" is one of Jupiter's moons. But it sounded close enough to me and I doubt many of the listeners knew much about the moons of Jupiter).

Billy continued. "I would go there because of its many unique features." We were now on a roll as Billy began to describe the many features as if he were Carl Sagan's long-lost brother.

I wasn't about to let Billy go. He was the only thing saving the program. It turned out Billy was a former aerospace engineer (if he wasn't, he certainly put on a good show that saved me for several minutes). I continued to ask him questions as if he were my intended guest.

Finally it was time to let my lone caller go. No one else called for the rest of the show. I still had eleven minutes until the conclusion of the program. By then I had passed a note to the producer to call a good friend of mine who worked in international development. He was at work and joined me over the phone to fill the few remaining minutes.

I still have the tape of that first talk show. Although I spend time on the radio, my talk show "experience" has come in a substitute role. But I learned early on the vital importance of having a back-up plan. I did not carry any resources into the studio that day, save the notes for my intended topic. Today, I always bring several newspapers with me and have a few magazine articles on hand if I am interviewed or if I must host a show. I can always begin to discuss an interesting topic I have found and generate some discussion on the airwaves.

Always have a back-up plan. Billy may not always be around to save the day.

"Life is a series of experiences, each one of which makes us bigger, even though it is hard to realize this. For the world was built to develop character, and we must learn that the setbacks and grieves which we endure help us in our marching onward."

—HENRY FORD

I t's one of the oldest and best-known companies in the music business, yet many people have never heard its name. It's not a record label or a recording studio, but if it were not for this factory in eastern Pennsylvania, some of the world's best-known songs would have not been played.

Today the sixth generation of the Martin family oversees the Martin Guitar Company in the small town of Nazareth. While the world around it has changed since it was founded in 1833, much of the skilled craftsmanship needed to make guitars remains just as it did when C. F. Martin founded his business.

Consider that many of the world's great singers and songwriters have played Martin guitars. Gene Autry, Willie Nelson, Eric Clapton, Elvis Presley, Paul Simon . . . the list goes on and on. What the Louisville Slugger bat company is to baseball is what the Martin Guitar Company is to the music world.

One of the best parts about the factory is the fact that it is open to the public. Before I sat down to interview George Molchany, one of the long-time craftsmen at Martin, he suggested that we take a quick look at the guitar-making process. Already knowing that so many famous musicians use instruments made here, I asked George, "What makes them choose a guitar from here instead of somewhere else? He simply replied, "Our guitars just sound the best."

That answer wasn't just a way to side-step my question, or a way to brag about having Grammy-winning musicians tour the factory. Musicians can tell a difference in the way guitars sound, and Martin takes great pride in fashioning the best in the business. George went on to back up his statement by telling me that producing great-sounding guitars is definitely not a quick process.

As he explained, there are over three hundred specific operations that have to be performed. Some of these operations are quite detailed and take much time. At one point in the process, you will still see hundreds of clothespins used to hold strips of lining onto the body of the guitars. Some intricate pearl inlay work may require a craftsman to spend well over ten hours on just one instrument.

This is the type of work where a sixteenth of an inch seems like a mile. Wood chisels and sandpaper are still very important tools of the trade. "Hand" work is the only type of work that will do in most cases. In fact, much of this process is still the same as it was when the company was founded back in 1833.

Probably the most important part of the entire process comes when the neck, or handle, of the guitar is fitted onto the body. The fit must be perfect in order for the guitar to play and sound its best. This requires fine rasps, files, and sandpaper.

Finally, the guitar reaches George. He is step number three hundred. This is a great position, because it is here that George becomes the first person to play the instrument. He smiled and said, "The guitar becomes a playable instrument in my hands and that is a good feeling. The pride alone when you see the finished product is very rewarding."

Most interesting to me is to hear George talk with his counterparts at "step 300." To an outsider, this just looks like a few guys picking away at new guitar strings. But when you step closer you hear George and the others say things like, "Play this one. The wood really brings out the bass tones." It's fun to listen to how their ears hear a unique sound from each instrument. They have spent so much time playing and building guitars, they know that each has its own unique sound.

Leadership is not a quick and easy process. Greatness is shaped and molded over years. Experience takes off the rough edges and helps us "get in tune" with others. After three hundred steps, a new Martin guitar has a unique sound regarded as tops in the industry. Time, experience, and patience are qualities sometimes overlooked in a fast-paced world, yet they are the very qualities that bring forth greatness. These qualities help shape unique people—and items—that have special qualities you just can't find anywhere else. As George says, "You just can't rush a good thing."

Chimney Rock

BAYARD, NEBRASKA

*"Go instead where there is no path and leave a trail.
Only those who will risk going too far can possibly
find out how far one can go."*

—T. S. ELIOT

G ordon Howard is a man who literally has the most important landmark on the Oregon Trail sitting in his backyard. In fact, of the thousands of immigrants who passed through western Nebraska following the Platte River on their way west, ninety-two percent of those keeping journals wrote about this spot. No other landmark was mentioned as many times as the "inverted funnel," a place more commonly known as Chimney Rock. To those early immigrants, this was *the* landmark on the trail.

When I met Howard, we stood in his yard and began to visit about this well-known spot on the old trail. He truly does live in the shadow of history, with Chimney Rock looming as a skyscraper on the Nebraska plains. Not only can he see history every day, but much of his life has been spent reliving the life of those pioneers. Howard related to me how he began the Oregon Trail Wagon Train, a business that operates authentic wagon train trips up and down the trail along the Platte River. The trips range from just a couple of days to a week or more, with each step of the way designed to imitate life in the mid 1800s.

Chimney Rock continues to draw onlookers today, but for pioneers it was truly a landmark to behold on what could be a long and difficult trip. Many of those headed toward Oregon and California would leave Missouri in late April or early May. By mid June they would be on the lookout for this chimney-like spire in the sky. Immigrant Joseph Hackney wrote, "This is the most remarkable object that I ever saw, and if situated in the states would be visited by persons from all parts of the world."

Howard noted that by the time people like Joseph Hackney reached Chimney Rock, they were leaving the prairie portion of their journey and heading toward the more mountainous stretch of the trail. Although the land here is still mostly a flat plain, a broken chain of bluffs along the river begins to signal the rough terrain soon to appear. From this point, another three to four months of travel still lie ahead.

It is difficult to estimate how many people passed here. Historians once believed the figure was about 350,000. Today it is estimated that from a half million to a million immigrants made the trip on the trail to the state of Oregon and many other locations in the western and northwestern U.S. Not all of those who passed Chimney Rock were impressed. Some longed for the comforts of the land they had left, and this 325-foot spire of clay and sandstone only served to remind them of the desolate land they found surrounding them. Pioneer Charles Preuss wrote, "This afternoon we sighted at a distance, the so-called Chimney Rock. Nothing new otherwise. Oh, if there were a tavern here! Toward evening we reached Chimney Rock and camped opposite it."

Even so, this place served as an important benchmark to be reached on the trip west. Diseases, accidents, and hostile Indians were all concerns. It is estimated that between four and six percent of those who began the journey did not live to see their destination. Howard told me that immigrant trains would have sighted the rock about three days before reaching it. It would remain in view for two days having passed it. It was truly the "signpost of the Plains," as Howard described it. After passing Chimney Rock, pioneers would also pass two other important landmarks: Scottsbluff, about twenty miles to the west, and Independence Rock, in central Wyoming. Both are mentioned numerous times in journals, indicating their importance as benchmarks on the trip west.

Today farms and ranches occupy most of the Nebraska panhandle, but the marks of the thousands who passed Chimney Rock are still visible. The ruts of wagon wheels that rolled here over 150 years ago serve as a reminder of the arduous journey of those who helped a young country stretch from the Atlantic to the Pacific. For those pioneers, places like Chimney Rock served as much more than curious sights along the trail. These were markers to be hoped for, signals that progress was being made toward the goal of a prosperous life in a land far away. This was a long, difficult, and dangerous journey, and reaching these markers meant more of those nearly two thousand miles were behind them.

I have yet to encounter a worthwhile journey in life that does not require a person to overcome difficult obstacles. Those worries and barriers are enough to keep many from even attempting the journey itself. Others wonder if there is a way to get where they want while avoiding the toil and pain. Is there a way to keep moving forward despite stress? How do we hold onto a hopeful attitude when tough times surround us?

As we look at the lives of these immigrants through their journals, I am reminded of the simple yet important idea of "markers of hope." These are points in our lives that give us the desire to push forward despite the difficulties surrounding us. For these wagon trains, Chimney Rock was a landmark that was visible long before they reached it. More importantly, it loomed on the horizon as a signal of hope and progress. With the strength of their families that often surrounded them and the hope gathered from these signposts of the Plains, trains of pioneers continued their push forward. Each spot served as a goal to be reached and a reward of progress toward the Pacific.

Each of us needs to identify such markers in our lives . . . places on the horizon that give us hope. We can also gain strength from the special people around us and take pride in what has already been accomplished. Together, these positive forces, past, present, and future, give us the will to keep going every day. They become markers, just like Chimney Rock. that help us blaze new trails of success.

Roy's Place

GAITHERSBURG, MARYLAND

"Alone we can do so little; together we can do so much."

—HELEN KELLER

I can spot them from the moment they answer my first question. Roy was going to be one of "those" guys. What do I mean? I asked the first question . . . and half an hour later I was still waiting to ask the second. That was all right with me though—his tale was so interesting, I would have forgotten what to ask as a second question anyway. What resulted was a wonderful evening around the dinner table at a restaurant called "Roy's Place."

Roy Passin began his restaurant with that simple but appropriate name in 1955. In the early years, his restaurant served mostly as a bar and drew a rough crowd at times. In fact, he once had to take a rowdy customer outside and attempt to beat some sense back into him. However, when Roy wrestled the man outside, he realized he didn't have anything with which to drive home his point. So, he just took off his own shoe and beat the man over the head with it. The shoe fight made an impression on the man. Roy insists such measures were necessary to keep order in the place.

Things have changed since then. Although there is still a bar, the clientele is usually well behaved. Today it's the menu that initially draws most people to Gaithersburg, but it's the good food that keeps them coming back.

When you go to some restaurants it may take you a while to order because you have to decide between a few very good meals. At Roy's, it takes a long time to order because the menu is so large. When you open up this menu, you will immediately get an idea of the amazing mind this chef possesses.

I felt a little embarrassed to have to continually tell my server that I was not yet ready to order. It wasn't that I couldn't decide what to order, it was the fact that I needed more time just to read everything. You see, Roy's menu lists over two hundred sandwiches from which to choose, each with very unique combinations of ingredients.

After a half hour of reading and a few consultations with my server, I finally settled on the "Pocahontas" sandwich (number 69 for short). The description of the sandwich read "lobster salad, ham, Swiss cheese, golden sauce, all broiled on choice of bread."

Maybe it's not that unusual, but number 71 on the menu, "Lassie's Revenge" (which the menu says was invented by "Ken L. Ration"), consists of "one knockwurst, provolone cheese, bacon, fried onions and baked beans on a hard roll." Most of Roy's sandwiches contain unusual names with whimsical tag lines. In fact, the menu follows up with item number 72, "Lassie's Double Revenge—flavor tested by Al Po."

Even after ordering, I pleaded to get to keep my menu just to read more of the wild combinations and unusual names. Roy's humor continued with "The Real Gasser," otherwise known as item number 111. It consists of "Broiled knockwurst, melted sharp cheese, onions and sweet relish on French bread." Or how about number 127? The "Daddy Warbucks" is made of "Beef tongue, Swiss cheese, cole slaw and Russian dressing" on your choice of bread, of course.

The menu also offers a "good cold sandwich" (item number 7). This consists of two stale pieces of bread wrapped about a freshly made ice cube (The sandwich was born when a slightly intoxicated customer insisted he be served a "good cold sandwich." Roy had heard enough and served him what later became sandwich number 7). Other light eaters might choose the "nothing burger," a sandwich consisting simply of two pieces of buttered bread.

Roy's menu became so popular that he soon found people were taking them home. Now the first page of the menu issues the warning, "If you'll stop stealing our menus, we'll stop slashing your tires." The menu just keeps going and going, filling your belly with laughter long before your delicious meal arrives.

"We are not a fast food outlet," Roy says. "People who must eat on the run will not be happy here. People who enjoy real food and are willing to wait for it are our kind of customers."

Over time it has become quite a tribute to have a sandwich named in your honor. There are sandwiches named after children, wives, mother-in-laws, dishwashers, bartenders, lawyers, and doctors. In fact, in the early 1990s, Roy had a large, benign stomach tumor removed. While he was resting in his hospital room, his surgeon came by to check on him. While the doctor performed his routine post-operative check-up, he seemed hesitant about something. After about five minutes he blurted out, "My wife said I shouldn't ask you this, but would you name a sandwich after me?"

Roy granted the doctor's request and thus was born sandwich number 179, "A Chirurgeon's Sandwich" (Roy likes to use creative spellings of words), made of avocado, crab salad, golden brisket, and golden sauce on your choice of bread.

Many of Roy's servers have worked here for a decade or two. You can order by number and they can immediately tell you the name of the sandwich and vice versa. Roy told me he didn't just sit down and try to dream up disgusting combinations of foods. Each sandwich is a creation of ingredients that he believes taste great together. He said, "I have a gift of knowing what flavors should combine in foods.

I have made very few mistakes with it." With nearly a half-century of sandwich-making experience, it certainly isn't just the novelty that keeps people coming back. It's great food that brings people here—the unusual combinations truly taste great.

The premise behind Roy's creations is a wonderful lesson for each of us. All great leaders look for ways to create unique and great tasting "sandwiches." They look for ways to bring out the strengths and talents of each person to find lasting solutions. That can take time. It's rarely a quick fix. However, what may initially look absurd may just have the makings of a great success. And, unlike sandwich ingredients, individuals often possess many talents, not just one "flavor" to be combined with others.

Leaders and sandwich makers are constantly working to bring the best ingredients together. It's a lesson to ponder as you spend an hour or so simply reading the menu and eating your good cold sandwich at Roy's Place.

Pudge Goes Pro
CANTON, OHIO

"Here lies a man who knew how to enlist
in his service better men than himself."

— TOMBSTONE OF ANDREW CARNEGIE

Before there was ever anything called the National Football League and decades before quarterbacks and running backs were paid thousands and then millions of dollars to play the game, there was a man named Pudge Heffelfinger.

If you want to get to the bottom of an important story dealing with the game of football, there is only one place to go . . . the Pro Football Hall of Fame in Canton, Ohio. The researchers there can direct you to stacks of books, magazines, football programs, and videos to help answer your questions. These archivists are often called upon by major sports networks and NFL teams themselves to perform important research. They also receive calls by ordinary citizens trying to settle barroom bets. In fact, they even fielded a call one time to determine the inseam measurement of a prominent quarterback. That seems to be the most unusual question that has ever been asked, and the usually sure-minded folks in Canton couldn't answer it.

If you want to find out about the beginnings of the game, you need to look back to the 1890s when athletic clubs in the northeastern U.S. fielded football teams to compete in a local circuit. The players were not paid, but the athletic clubs would do just about anything to get the best players on their teams. Plenty of money was riding on these early games.

Although league rules strictly forbid the paying of players, clubs were known to give a nice watch to a player who'd had a particularly great day on the field. The gift could then be pawned for cash. Other teams might find a good paying job for a player. Still others used the practice of paying double expense money. Each method was designed to be a "legal" way to compensate the players.

For many years, the Pro Football Hall of Fame here in Canton believed a sixteen-year-old quarterback named John Brallier became the first pro football player when he accepted ten dollars to play in a game for Latrobe, Pennsylvania, in 1895. However, after further research, the Hall of Fame would find documents to prove otherwise.

In the fall of 1892, the Allegheny Athletic Association (AAA) was set to play its rival, the Pittsburgh Athletic Club (PAC). The two teams had battled to a 6-6 tie earlier in the season. Pittsburgh's star player, William Kirschner, was injured. Both the AAA and PAC were looking to stock their rosters with top talent.

Earlier that year, the Chicago Athletic Club, behind the talent of Pudge Heffelfinger, had rolled to an easy victory over Cleveland. News reports stated that the PAC had offered Heffelfinger and other Chicago players as much as $250 to play against the AAA. Their efforts to sign the players had failed.

When the PAC and AAA took to the field November 12, 1892, the PAC was amazed to look across the field to see Heffelfinger and a few other Chicago athletes wearing AAA uniforms. Wagering on the game was immediately suspended. The PAC walked off the field and the AAA was accused of paying players. Finally the two teams agreed to play the game as an exhibition. The game was shortened to two thirty-minute halves, instead of the usual forty-five minutes per half. All of the arguing meant the teams would have to hurry to finish the game before sundown.

Many years later, the Allegheny Athletic Association's expense sheet would be uncovered. It would show that Pudge Heffelfinger had been paid the extraordinarily high sum of $500 in cash to play that day. Other players had been given double expense money or other means of "non-cash" payments to play. The AAA's payment of Heffelfinger was well worth the money. Pudge forced a fumble in the first half, picked up the ball, and rumbled into the end zone for a touchdown. In 1892, a touchdown was worth four points. That's exactly where the score remained, with the AAA defeating the PAC 4-0.

Pudge was an outstanding football player, but he never caught a touchdown pass. Then again, no one caught any passes until 1906, when the forward pass was first allowed. Even then, grid markings were placed on the field and many limitations were written into the rules so that passing didn't take over the game. Today, at the Football Hall of Fame, you can see the accounting sheet that clearly shows Pudge's $500 payment, putting him in the books as the first recorded professional football player.

Not only was this an historic moment, it shows the importance of surrounding yourself with the right players. Although we certainly must compete within the rules, the value of talent and experience to help a team can be invaluable. For Pudge Heffelfinger, that talent was enough to put him in the score book and the history book and start a trend of highly paid athletes that lives on today.

Project Greek Island

WHITE SULPHUR SPRINGS, WEST VIRGINIA

*"The quality of a person's life is in direct proportion
to their commitment to excellence, regardless
of their chosen field of endeavor."*

—VINCE LOMBARDI

As Americans celebrated the end of war in 1945, many did not realize how the events of that year would change life forever. The use of nuclear weapons in Japan created a threat that could impact the lives of thousands with the use of one single weapon. Soon the Soviet Union possessed the same weapons of mass destruction and the superpowers settled in for what would become known as the Cold War.

With the advent of the nuclear age, the U.S. government took steps to protect its very existence. Bunkers and fall-out shelters were constructed across the nation to protect citizens. No project may have been as large and secretive as the one that took place in the mountains of West Virginia. It was a plan simply known as Project Greek Island.

By the mid-1950s a large bunker was needed to house the U.S. Congress in case of nuclear attack. The search for a secret location within driving range of Washington, D.C., led to the luxurious Greenbrier Resort in White Sulphur Springs. The decision was made to build a large underground bunker on the grounds of the resort. The only problem was how to construct an 112,000-square-foot facility without anyone knowing of its existence.

The hotel offered a cover story. In 1958, construction began on a new, three-story addition to the hotel called the West Virginia Wing. While floors began moving upward, excavation moved downward. Construction crews didn't realize what they were building. The underground portions of the building were billed as an exhibit hall. They could also double as a fall-out shelter. (It wasn't uncommon to build such shelters at that time.) Ironically, hotel guests even used portions of the secret bunker without realizing they were in it.

There were four entrances to the bunker, each sealed by a twenty-five-ton door that was eighteen inches thick. The facility was built to accommodate about 1,100 people for up to sixty days. Approximately 700-800 of those occupants would have been legislators and their staffs. While accommodations above ground were lavish, Congress would have experienced a basic existence in its bunker. Eighteen dormitories on two levels could house sixty people each.

Two meeting rooms were maintained just off the hotel's main exhibit hall. Governor's Hall and the Mountaineer Room would have served as a temporary home for the Senate and House of Representatives. About a dozen government employees worked at the Greenbrier and were in charge of maintaining the bunker. They were employees of a cover business called Forsythe Associates. The group was in charge of audio-visual needs at the resort and performed routine maintenance needs such as television repair. About twenty percent of the crew's time was actually spent on hotel maintenance with the remaining eighty percent used to keep the bunker ready for use by the government.

The bunker might still be "in use" today if it were not for a story printed by the *Washington Post* in May of 1992. It disclosed the

Greenbrier as the probable location for a secret bunker to house Congress. For over three decades, the handful of employees at Forsythe Associates had performed their duties faithfully. Only their spouses were allowed to know what they really did at the Greenbrier. These families could not even tell their children about the project. To them, they were simply TV repair people at a fancy resort.

Some people view Project Greek Island as a waste of tax money. Others see it as a necessary cost of being a superpower nation during the cold war. Both sides may be right. However, to me, the people I admire in this story are the people who spent each day faithfully working for Forsythe. They were loyal to their country and kept quiet in order to assist their nation. Thankfully, their hard work keeping the bunker ready was never needed. To others, they were simply fixing television sets at the resort.

Loyalty is a very important part of leadership. Many times that loyalty does not seem to pay any dividends. For employees here, their loyalty to their country was not known for over three decades. That certainly does not mean they didn't play a very important part in our nation's security, though.

We sometimes believe our work always has to be rewarded. However, some of the greatest and most important jobs in life may require the recognition of our hard work to take a back seat, so to speak. That does not mean the task is not important. To the contrary, it may just be one of the most important services you can give to others. That was definitely the case for the employees at Forsythe who secretly worked at Project Greek Island and faithfully served their nation for over three decades.

One Vote

GREENEVILLE, TENNESSEE

"One man with courage makes a majority."

— ANDREW JACKSON

The line between courageousness and stupidity may be difficult to discern. Such was the case for two men facing tough political decisions just after the close of the Civil War. Many ridiculed their decisions, but the stand they took is still a lesson to leaders today.

The story began in Greeneville, Tennessee, a small town in the eastern part of the Volunteer State, when young Andrew Johnson moved here to open a tailor shop. Ironically, the tailor trade was something he ran away from home to avoid during his teenage years. Johnson's father died when he was just a child, and his mother apprenticed him to a local tailor so that young Andrew would have a career someday. She never imagined that the new career would provide him with the skills to lead him all the way to the White House.

By his mid twenties, Andrew Johnson had built a good business and a good reputation here at the corner of College and Depot streets. His tailor shop was well run and well visited. He was much more than a tailor; he was actually educating himself in several different careers, all at the same time. He hired people to read books to him as he worked and always made time to talk with the many political leaders who stopped by his store. Andrew Johnson was constantly around the news of the day and he was making an effort to continually keep abreast of the world of politics.

Although the tailor shop was successful, Johnson longed to run for political office and soon set his sights on the position of city alderman. Later, he worked up the political ranks, serving as mayor of Greeneville. There were bigger offices to run for, and the tailor shop was eventually left behind as he became a state representative, then governor of Tennessee, and finally a U.S. senator.

Johnson was serving in the U.S. Senate when southern states seceded from the Union. Although Johnson was a democrat from a slave-holding state, he sought to preserve the union. In fact, when all other southern U.S. senators left Congress in favor of succession, Johnson did not leave. It was a courageous decision, but a decision not without consequences. The move made him a hero in the eyes of the north, but a traitor in the eyes of many southerners. When Johnson returned home to Tennessee in 1861, he barely escaped a lynch mob as he rode the train through Virginia. Tensions were high and war was beginning to rip the union apart. Every decision would be met by fierce opposition from one side or the other. Now was the time to know what one believed in and stood for.

Johnson stood by his decision to remain in the Congress. "I intend to stand by the Constitution as it is, insisting upon a compliance with all its guaranties . . . it is the last hope of human freedom," he declared.

In 1862, Lincoln appointed Johnson military governor of Tennessee. Two years later, in 1864, Lincoln selected Johnson as his vice presidential candidate. The two handily won the presidential election. Barely into his second term of office, on April 15, 1865, Lincoln was assassinated and the democrat from Greeneville, Tennessee, was sworn in as the seventeenth president of the United States.

Johnson was immediately thrust into a position in which there was no way to "win." There was bitter debate over how to reconstruct the South. Johnson opposed the views of staunch republicans in Congress and vetoed much of their legislation. In an effort to control the actions of the president, Congress passed the Tenure of Office Act. The provision stated that a president could not dismiss a member of his cabinet without the approval of Congress. Johnson did not believe the act was constitutional and fired his Secretary of War Edwin Stanton and appointed Ulysses S. Grant in his place. Johnson had not even appointed Stanton to the position; he had inherited his cabinet from Lincoln. Stanton refused to give up his position and was reinstated by the Senate in January of 1868.

One month later, Johnson once again fired Stanton. Congress was furious. They brought eleven articles of impeachment against Johnson for "high crimes and misdemeanors." In order to remove the president from office, two-thirds of the Senate had to vote for his conviction. The trail began in March of 1868 and lasted two months.

The vote was a virtual deadlock. Johnson's opponents needed thirty-six votes to remove him from office. It appeared Johnson's opponents were one vote short, but one senator was still undecided . . . Senator Edmund Ross from Kansas. Ross did not announce his intentions until his name was called to state his vote. Ross rose and simply replied, "Not guilty."

That one vote was enough to keep Johnson in office. That one vote also spelled the end of Ross' political career. Republicans were infuriated that he would support Johnson and Ross was never elected to another office.

Today that vote is considered a courageous vote of foresight. If Johnson had been removed, it would have set a precedent that Congress could pass unpopular legislation and use it to remove a president from office. Ross saw the larger picture. His vote was costly though. He was ostracized and attacked in his home state of Kansas. He was unable to gain reelection and he died in poverty.

Johnson was certainly courageous in standing up for his view on how the reconstruction of the union should proceed. Certainly there was fault on both sides. Johnson can be admired for not wavering during a time when strong leadership was needed. Johnson sought reelection in 1868 but was not even nominated by his own party. Horatio Seymour of New York became the democratic candidate. Ulysses S. Grant, the man Johnson had sought to make secretary of war, defeated Seymour.

Today, most people do not even know there is a tailor shop here in Greeneville where young Andrew Johnson learned his early lessons of leadership. However, the place marks the spot where a president would take his first steps toward the White House. It was a presidency preserved by a Kansas senator named Ross. The two would make history for their courageous votes during a difficult time. It's a lesson that still stands today.

"You can turn painful situations around through laughter. If you can find humor in anything—even poverty—you can survive it."

—BILL COSBY

M att had a dream like many other young men entering college. . . . He wanted to marry a college cheerleader. One great route to accomplishing that feat is to be a superstar athlete. Matt was athletic, but not nearly skilled enough to make any of the teams at Oklahoma State University. So, when Matt couldn't make one of the teams, there was only one route to spend time around the cheerleaders . . . become the mascot.

Pistol Pete is the mascot of Oklahoma State University. Matt saw an advertisement in the school newspaper inviting anyone interested in becoming the mascot to attend an informational meeting and try-outs. He thought he would attend the tryouts and get the experience he would need to make a serious run at the title for next year. It didn't take a "next year" for Matt. He was selected to become Pistol Pete on his very first try.

Life on the road can be dangerous for mascots. One of the most notorious spots on Pistol Pete's tour is my alma mater, the University of Missouri. I was there for the game when the Missouri cheerleaders captured poor Pete and began to carry him around the field. As if that weren't bad enough, things got worse when the Missouri cheerleaders put Pete in a "spread eagle" position and rammed him into the goal post!

Matt was not yet playing the role of Pete when that incident occurred, but he did draw the short straw to come to Missouri the next year. He had heard the reports from the game the year before and knew that things might get out of hand in Columbia, Missouri. His fears were confirmed when one of the security guards at the game that day saw Pete (Matt) before the game and warned him, "The last three mascots that came here were rammed into the goal post. Watch out!"

Matt knew that if there were trouble, there would be little he could do to defend himself, so he warned the OSU cheerleaders to be on the look out for any suspicious activity. If anything happened, they would run to his aid.

The first half of the MU/OSU football game was uneventful for Pete. It was a nice afternoon and everything seemed to be running smoothly for the OSU cheerleaders and their mascot. The halftime show had just begun, with the Missouri marching band taking to the field. Little did Pete know that Missouri was attempting to make him a part of the show.

A man came up behind Matt and said, "Hey, Pistol Pete, this little girl over here wants to shake your hand." Matt, wearing the forty-five-pound Pistol Pete head, looked in the direction the man pointed. He didn't see any little girl.

It was a set up. With Matt's attention diverted, the Missouri cheerleaders swooped in behind Matt and picked him up, carrying him above their heads toward the goal post.

The Missouri cheerleaders, with Pistol Pete in tow, were heading for the end of the field and the goalpost. They were ready to chalk up their fourth victim of the season. OSU's squad spotted the melee and ran to track down the attackers and thwart the scheme. In the meantime, Matt was reaching for his pistol. Sure, it's a mascot pistol, but he could still use the fake six-shooter to beat the cheerleaders over the head.

In the brawl that ensued, it was all Matt could do to keep Pete's head on top of his own head. One of a mascot's biggest fears is to have the fake head ripped off, revealing his or her true identity. During the scuffle between the two teams' cheerleaders, Matt held on to the inside of Pete's head, doing everything he could to keep it from rolling onto the field.

No one remembers the outcome of the football game, but everyone remembers that OSU pulled the upset that day as they squelched Missouri's attempt to introduce another mascot to the goalpost. It was Matt's most eventful appearance as the mascot.

During two years of work as Pistol Pete, Matt made over six hundred appearances. Although his goal of marrying a cheerleader did not come true, the experience gave him a unique look on life . . . a set of experiences that influence his life today.

Matt says of being a mascot, "It's truly an art form. It's difficult to make people laugh because mascots don't talk." In fact, many mascots spend a portion of their summer at "mascot school" where they learn some of the do's and don'ts of their line of work.

The biggest thrill to Matt was simply looking for ways to bring a smile to people's faces. He developed several gigs that would grab some laughs, but noted that it takes time to think of what to do. "When you're a mascot, you've got to tell the story through your actions," he reminds.

"People come to the games with different feelings, problems, or concerns. The opportunity to go up and shake somebody's hand, give them a big hug, or pull a little prank on them seemed to help them forget about whatever their worries were and help them just laugh and have a good time."

Study after study has shown the life-giving power of laughter. In fact, some medical programs today make use of comedy because of the healing power laughter can have on a person's body. While we should never neglect the seriousness of the task at hand, we each can work to bring a smile and a laugh to people. It is an art that Matt has studied through his role as Pistol Pete. It is a role each of us should implement in our daily lives as well.

Hindenburg

LAKEHURST, NEW JERSEY

"The years teach us much the days never knew."

—RALPH WALDO EMERSON

Some people would call me a road warrior. I have a frequent flier account with just about every airline, and even some that are now bankrupt. I can set foot in about any U.S. airport terminal and tell you where the nearest restroom is located. I even know that seat 8C on an Embraer 120 turboprop is the best seat on the commuter plane because it has triple the amount of normal legroom. That's scary!

I am actually at home much more than I am on the road, but my occasional flights do earn me several frequent flyer miles each year. One "perk" of such traveling is that you can cash in those miles for free tickets. Those tickets can come in handy for a family member who may need to travel at the last minute for an emergency. Sometimes I will give my parents a couple of tickets so they can take a vacation. However, I rarely use the miles for my own leisure. After I've been on the road for a long time, the last thing I want to do is cash in my frequent flier miles to leave and go somewhere else. So, in 2001, I used only one free ticket for a special trip to a wonderful location over Labor Day weekend. Where? The Navy Lakehurst Historical Society Picnic.

For those who know their history, Lakehurst, New Jersey, is synonymous with the Hindenburg airship disaster in 1937. The local historical society even holds their annual picnic at the Lakehurst Naval Air Center, site of the crash. That's where I traveled on the first day of September to visit with John Ianacone, the last member of the ground crew who is still living today.

"In 1936 it made ten round trips here," he said as we sat down under a large picnic shelter and began to eat our meal of hot dogs, chips, and soda.

John was there for those landings in 1936. The first of those trans-Atlantic trips landed at Lakehurst on the morning of May 9, 1936. It took over sixty-one hours to fly from Germany to New Jersey. Over the next three days, Hindenburg was moored in hangar number one at the Air Center and an estimated seventy-five thousand visitors came to see the craft during an open house. John was one of those who managed to get a tour of the eight hundred-foot-long Hindenburg.

It was one of the most impressive things he had ever seen. "It had two promenade decks in there. They (the German crew) showed us the galley. It was all electric. They even had a piano."

Space was limited on the large ship though. Passenger cabins measured a mere 78 × 66 inches. Crew quarters were also very tight. Passengers could enjoy the larger promenade area where they could get a panoramic view of the earth and seas below. They could also enjoy the smoking room, an ironic addition to a craft inflated with highly flammable hydrogen. Hindenburg could carry about fifty passengers and another fifty crew. The return trip of Hindenburg to Frankfurt took less time than the maiden crossing, traversing the distance in forty-eight and a half hours.

Of course, John's job was not to take tours of the Hindenburg but to help secure it upon landing. The nose of the craft was attached to a mooring mast, but the tail was allowed to move with the wind.

"The tail would sit on this little flat car so that it could go around like a weather vane so that nobody would have to watch it. They would only stay here a few hours; they would come in at six or seven o'clock in the morning and leave at eleven o'clock at night," he explained.

As John and I downed the last of our hotdogs and chips, he worked to get me to understand how the events unfolded that fateful evening in 1937. Soon, we were using our now empty paper cups to represent the mooring mast and our paper plates had become the flatcar on which the tail of the Hindenburg would rest.

May 6, 1937, was an overcast day. This was to be the first of eighteen scheduled round trips from Germany to the U.S. that year. The ship was carrying thirty-six passengers and sixty-one crew members. Strong headwinds delayed the trip so that Hindenburg could not make its usual morning landing. The approach was delayed until about seven o'clock. The peaceful evening was soon turned to a half minute of sheer terror.

"We could see the whole thing from the nose back to the tail. When it caught on fire there was a big red glow inside just forward of the tail and then it broke through the fabric and started to burn. It took thirty-four seconds from the time the fire started to the time it was completely burned and on the ground. It actually didn't crash; it just settled to the ground."

Despite the fact that the Hindenburg was a falling fireball, John's reaction was to see what he could do to save lives. "We started to run toward the ship and see if we could help with anybody. We got to the nose before anybody else. As the nose hit the ground, one man walked out. He didn't have a stitch of clothes on him. His shoes, his hair, his skin was all burned off. He died before they got him to an ambulance."

Herb Morrison provided the lone radio account of the tragedy. Many will remember his famous line "Oh the humanity!" as the airship went down in flames. Hindenburg burst into flame almost two hundred feet above the ground before its gentle yet fiery decent at the mooring circle. Thirty-six people died in the disaster that evening: thirteen passengers, twenty-two crew, and one ground crew member.

It all happened so fast. An airship eight hundred feet long was gone in half a minute. The event would not only mark the end of the Hindenburg, it would also conclude the use of airships for commercial travel. The cause of the disaster is still not known, although many theories have been offered. John believes static electricity from the mooring cable may have ignited hydrogen as it was vented from the ship.

A simple marker has been placed where the tragedy unfolded that night. The historical society remembers those who lost their lives by hosting a memorial service each May 6, at 7:25 P.M., the time of the crash.

As John and I concluded our history lesson and placed our model of the landing site in the trash, the historical society gathered for their annual picture. They even invited me to jump in and be a part of it. It was a nice conclusion to a wonderful day. I really felt like I was part of their group.

One important lesson I've learned through my radio broadcasts is the value of recording the stories of previous generations. In fact, I've made an effort to search out people like John who have unique stories to tell. Sometimes we never think about recording those stories until it is too late. Sometimes spending time "just listening" is some of the most valuable time we can spend. We learn so much that we can apply in our own lives and share with generations to come. It's generational leadership, passing down the important stories and truths of life to others.

That's why it made perfect sense to me to fly to Lakehurst and be a part of a picnic. I hope you, too, will take time to learn from those generations around you and share their stories with generations to follow.

Cal Farley

Boys Ranch, Texas

"We make a living by what we get,
but we make a life by what we give."

— Winston Churchill

In the beginning, Cal Farley's love of sports may have been born more out of necessity than a true liking for games. His older brother was known to wrestle with Cal, who was much smaller and younger, and he soon had to learn ways to keep from ending up on the bottom of the heap every single time. Cal found out that what he gave up in size, he gained back through speed. He soon began to use his small stature to his advantage, not only to wrestle against his older brother but also others in the small town of Sexton, Iowa, where he was raised.

As Cal's wrestling skills grew, he began to promote wrestling matches in neighboring towns. He would travel to those locations to take on the strongest opponents the towns could supply. He did so well that he was able to live mostly off the earnings from winning those matches. By 1917, though, the setting and type of competition had changed. Cal enlisted in the army and was sent to France to fight in World War I. This time, in the face of a life and death "match" on the battlefield, he fought valiantly and was one of only thirty-four men to survive from his original company of 250 men.

As U.S. forces were waiting to be sent back home to the States with the close of war in 1918, games were organized to provide competition for the restless troops. Cal signed up to wrestle and advanced all the way to the championship match played in Paris with General Pershing in the audience.

In what has been called one of the most amazing examples of strength and courage in sports, Cal overcame the extreme pain of a badly cut knee to take down his opponent with only eighteen seconds remaining in the thirty-minute championship match. The pain caused him to pass out just as he claimed victory and when he finally awoke, he found his opponent holding him under a shower trying to revive him. Cal Farley returned home a victor in war and a victor in the wrestling ring. But he was ready to help make others victors in the game of life.

In 1923, Cal's sports interest turned to baseball. While playing in the minor leagues in Amarillo, he began to notice the many youngsters who would flock to the games. What bothered him was the fact that many of these kids didn't seem to have anywhere to go except to the ball game. Often, these kids came from broken homes and didn't have families who could adequately care for them. Cal wanted to do something for these young fans that would make a lasting difference in their lives.

After building a successful tire business during the heart of the depression, he acquired 120 acres of ranch land about forty miles northwest of Amarillo. That small acreage was the beginning of what is today Cal Farley's Boys Ranch. The first nine boys came to live there in 1939, on the site of the old county seat of Tascosa. A ghost town, a crew soon renovated the old courthouse into sleeping quarters and began to slowly expand from there.

Cal's dream was to build a place "for the bottom ten percent of America's youth." He was known to travel over three thousand miles to pick up a troubled young man after a judge had contacted the ranch as a possible home for the misguided youth. It was all a part of the effort to instill in these young men the "three D's" as he called them—desire, determination, and dedication.

A big boost came in 1944 when the *Saturday Evening Post* ran an article about Boys Ranch. Soon celebrities like Roy Rogers and Dale Evans gave their support. More homes and classrooms were built, more land was acquired, and more boys called Boys Ranch "home." The famous Boys Ranch Rodeo also began. The annual event is open to students at the ranch and attracts visitors from across the country still today.

It was always Cal Farley's belief that many of the juveniles destined for penitentiaries could be molded into productive leaders if there was a good home where they could be raised. Boys Ranch still tries to accomplish that difficult task. Cal once said, "The wildest colts make the best horses if properly trained." Ironically, many of the students at Boys Ranch (although the name has remained "Boys Ranch," girls are now a part of the school as well) learn life lessons by breaking colts themselves. The ranch is now ten thousand acres in size and horses are an important part of the operation. Caring for horses and other animals has become a way for many of these students to begin to realize their responsibility to care for others. A wild colt and a "wild" student in a sense are learning about life together.

Boys Ranch is open to visitors and, since Cal's death in 1967, almost half a million visitors have come here. More importantly, young men and women leave with a strong education and a new outlook on life. Boys Ranch alumni are well-respected members of their communities. Cal's life was built on the three principles of desire, determination, and dedication and those same qualities are helping Boys Ranch graduates succeed in life.

When you enter the ranch you will pass under an archway with the famous words "Cal Farley's Boys Ranch—A Shirttail to Hang Onto." This is a special place that allows people to grab hold of hope. How important a caring attitude and a sense of hope can be in a person's life, for here it is the recipe that turns lives around every day. It is exemplified in the teachers and staff who work here and it is passed on to each student. As Cal Farley said, "It is easy to smile when someone cares."

Reverend Taylor, the Marriage Man
GATLINBURG, TENNESSEE

*"I don't know what your destiny will be, but one thing I know;
the only ones among you who will be really happy are those who
have sought and found how to serve."*

— ALBERT SCHWEITZER

There was no doubt about it . . . Reverend Taylor had to be a real kook.

That's what I thought when I rolled into Gatlinburg, Tennessee, a beautiful little town at the western entrance of Smokey Mountain National Park. Revered Ed Taylor came here in the late 1970s to set up a tourist ministry. It was a logical location to reach lots of people since Smokey Mountain National Park is the most visited national park in the nation.

Soon after his arrival in Gatlinburg, Rev. Taylor learned that hundreds of couples were coming to Gatlinburg to get married. Area churches did not want to marry people who were just passing through town, so couples simply went to the local justice of the peace to perform the ceremony. Those wedding ceremonies often made a mockery of the institution of marriage, with ceremonies taking place in feed and seed stores.

Taylor decided that something had to be done to restore dignity and sanctity to these services. These couple needed to have a good beginning to their lives together. Although a pastor does much more than marry people, Taylor saw there was a great need for an ordained minister to help these couples have a respectable and Godly marriage service. So, he began to perform marriage ceremonies, providing an alternative to couples who once had no choice but to go to the local justice of the peace.

Rev. Taylor never imagined the industry he would help create. The "wedding business" is now the third largest industry in Sevier County. Gatlinburg ranks second only to Las Vegas in the number of marriage ceremonies performed each year. Many wedding chapels have opened in town, but Rev. Taylor established the very first one. By the beginning of the year 2001, Rev. Taylor had married 85,000 couples in his lifetime. He is believed to have married more couples than any other person in the world!

During his tenure as a pastor here in Gatlinburg, Rev. Taylor has even married a few celebrities. Well-known singers like Billy Ray Cyrus have had Rev. Taylor perform their marriage ceremonies and sports stars such as Dan Marino have been guests at his services. Over the years, this small chapel has grown so that it can host more than one wedding at a time. The great number of weddings has not diminished the importance or dignity of the services, but added chapels do allow Rev. Taylor to marry more couples.

Rev. Taylor says the word "marriage" is derived from the word "one." It was many years later that the word "wedding" came into usage. "Wedding" comes from the word "celebration." He saw a lot of people getting "wed" without getting "married." So his goal was to start newlyweds on the right track.

"Couples who worship together and pray together are couples who are likely to stay together," he says. His counseling and marriage services guide couples in making this happen. The goal is to help couples lay the groundwork for a marriage that will last a lifetime. And that is a very worthy goal in light of the high percentage of marriages today that end in divorce.

Nothing seems to please Taylor more than when couples return several years later to thank him for the time he took to get their marriage off to the right start. Although it is difficult to stay in touch with every couple he marries, Taylor hears of few that ever decide to split. Taylor guides these couples in developing a solid foundation for their marriages, and that commitment makes a lasting difference.

Initially, I had figured that any man who performed weddings at this pace had to be a kook. I was mistaken. Rev. Taylor taught me an important lesson. He shared with me a favorite quote from Norman Vincent Peale: "Find the need and fill it, find the hurt and heal it, find the problem and solve it." That quote was and still is Rev. Taylor's inspiration as he performs each ceremony.

What a powerful statement. In a place where hundreds of people are married every day, Rev. Taylor is not in this for money or to set a record. He is determined to counsel every couple he meets to help make sure their marriage lasts for a lifetime. Rev. Taylor is filling needs, healing hurts, and solving problems. How well do we accomplish that task in our lives? It's a task to which everyone should say, "I do."

Diseased Network?
LOUISVILLE, KENTUCKY

"Press on: Nothing in the world can take the place of perseverance. Talent will not; nothing is more common than unsuccessful men with talent. Genius will not; unrewarded genius is almost a proverb. Education will not; the world is full of educated derelicts. Persistence and determination alone are omnipotent."

—CALVIN COOLIDGE

Sometimes you have to give a guy a lift. Dick didn't have a car at the airport, so I went to pick him up. What resulted was a memorable conversation with a memorable man of sports.

It's a very short drive from Louisville's Standiford Field to Freedom Hall arena. However, when I pulled up the car to pick up Dick Vitale, I knew that the few minutes would be packed with plenty of excitement. His smile and "Hi, how are ya?" were just what one would expect from the well-known ESPN commentator.

Part of my job that day was to pick up Vitale and take him to the hall for a speaking engagement. The other part of the job was to interview him and learn more about his life story. During our visit in the car and in our interview, I learned so much about how to deal with life's obstacles. Vitale's enthusiasm is enough to motivate just about anyone. When you hear his story, it serves as a double-dose of energy.

Vitale's rise to basketball prominence came very quickly. In 1970 Dick Vitale was teaching the sixth grade. The very next year he made the jump to the collegiate ranks, becoming an assistant basketball coach at Rutgers University. By 1973 he had moved from Rutgers to the University of Detroit, where he became head coach. After success there, he moved on to a bigger job in the same city. In 1977 he was named head coach of the Detroit Pistons. As he notes, "In less than seven years I went from teaching sixth grade to being a head coach in the NBA."

It was a fairy tale of success, at least up to this point. Vitale's coaching fortunes with the Pistons would soon turn sour. Losses began to mount during his stint as coach and on November 8, 1979, that happily-ever-after tale took a very difficult turn. It was on that day that Vitale was fired as head coach of the Pistons. He was crushed. He went home and "lived in a shell," watching soap operas and rarely showing his face in public. He reflects, "I think that was the one time I violated everything I believed in."

A few weeks later, Vitale received a phone call that, at the time, didn't seem special at all. The head of production for a new sports network called ESPN remembered Vitale from his college coaching days and wanted the recently fired NBA coach to be a color commentator for their first game, DePaul versus Wisconsin. Vitale responded, "First of all what is ESPN? It sounds like a disease. I've never heard of it. Are you kiddin' me? I don't want to do that. I want to coach in college."

It took his wife Lorraine to give him a jolt. "Here's the one time in your life that things didn't go well and what you are doing is absolutely ludicrous," she said. "You're not doing anything. Just go out and have fun." At the time, Vitale reflects that he was only leaving his home to go to church. He took her advice. He did the

Depaul/Wisconsin game. He was paid $350 per game to do the color commentary for ESPN.

Vitale says that ESPN liked three qualities he brought to the broadcast. He provided knowledge, candidness, and enthusiasm. Today millions of viewers tune in to watch basketball games but also to hear Vitale deliver those same three qualities. His unique style and love for life have made him a bigger celebrity than many of the stars playing the game. When you hear and see Vitale on television, his style is far different than any other broadcaster's. Yet what you hear is purely how Vitale talks and thinks in everyday life. That genuine love for life and love for basketball has translated into loyal fans who tune in to see what he has to say.

Vitale inspires groups of students and adults on the speaking circuit as well. He says, "You gotta have faith when things get tough." Perseverance and enthusiasm are two important qualities he found to lift him during those difficult times. Obstacles and failures are a part of everyone's life. Some choose to crawl into a shell and never venture out again. Others learn the lesson Lorraine Vitale taught her husband in November of 1979. Even when times are tough and the pain is great, leaders get back out there and look for new ways to achieve. If Dick Vitale had chosen not to do that, he might be the world's best authority on soap operas instead of the top commentator in college basketball today.

Inside Out

ADA, OHIO

"What you are speaks so loudly I cannot hear what you say."

—RALPH WALDO EMERSON

The building is certainly ordinary. Its 1940's cinder block construction makes it look like many other factories in the Midwest. Ironically, what happens inside this building is far more than ordinary . . . it is magical. What is made inside these walls brings the cheers and boos of thousands, for this is the factory that makes NFL footballs.

Since the inception of the National Football League, Wilson Sporting Goods has supplied the official NFL football. Every point scored in an NFL game has been scored with a Wilson football. I arrived for my visit during mid December, a slower time for the employees here as the football season is winding down. Some footballs were still waiting to be shipped to stadiums in Florida and Texas where they would appear in college bowl games. The logos of those many games and teams had already been stamped on the balls and they sat boxed and ready for shipment.

Most people don't realize the amount of skilled labor that goes into making a football. The process takes time and precision. First, four leather panels are cut from a hide of specially tanned leather (the title "pigskin" is a misnomer) and the panels are stamped with the appropriate markings for its intended use. For example, some footballs will receive the logos of high school athletic associations. Others will get a college trademark. Still others receive the stamp "NFL."

Those four panels are sewn together, creating the first glimpse of what these slices of leather will become. Next, a three-ply lining is sewn into the football to protect the air bladder and help the ball retain its shape. All of the stitching is performed by hand; there really is no other way to put the parts of a football together. Its odd, leathery shape can't be created by a machine.

Most people do not realize that when constructing a football, most of the assembly is performed with the football turned inside out. This is done so that all of the stitches are on the inside of the football instead of the outside. One of the most difficult parts of the process is "turning" the football. Each "turner" has a steam box that they use to heat the leather to make it more pliable for turning. They also have iron bars to give them leverage in the turning process. Once the steam has made the leather more flexible, workers use those iron bars to turn the football, so the brown leather panels are now facing outward.

When the football is turned, its logos are once again visible. An air bladder is inserted, the football is double laced, and the ball is inflated and inspected. It is now ready to be boxed and shipped. A Wilson football has never failed in an NFL game. That is a fact these employees are very proud to share.

In one area of this small factory are the most important footballs of all . . . the Superbowl footballs. The night of the AFC and NFC championship games is a very hectic time. The logos of the Superbowl teams can't be placed on the footballs, of course, until the two league's champions have been crowned. Depending on the year, there are only one to two weeks between that game and the Superbowl. Wilson employees will work throughout the night stamping footballs with the correct match-up. It's a quick turn-around time to get the footballs to the title game.

About one hundred footballs are shipped to the stadium for potential use in the game with thousands more footballs shipped for sale as collector's items. Superbowl Sunday is kind of like Thanksgiving Day to these employees. It is a time to sit down and enjoy the fruits of labor. These employees know that no matter who wins or loses, all the points scored in this game have been scored with a product they made.

The part of the process that continues to stand out to me is the turning of the football. I had never realized that a football was constructed from the inside out. This principle is necessary to make a Superbowl football, and I sincerely hope each of us will look at constructing our own lives just as a football is manufactured.

Like a football, a leader must be built from the inside out. There is no other way. A leader needs to possess qualities such as a sense of integrity, a heart of loyalty, a desire to serve, and a willingness to listen—qualities found on the "inside."

The making of a championship football and a championship leader is exactly the same—from the inside out. George Burns once said the secret of great acting is sincerity. "If you can fake that," he said, "you've got it made." The comic contradiction by Burns is, unfortunately, advice many leaders try to take. A person's character cannot be faked for a lifetime. It's the single most important part of a person. Show me a leader's "insides" and I can tell if they are the leader for me.

Witches

SALEM, MASSACHUSETTS

"A good name is rather to be chosen than great riches."

—PROVERBS 22:1

Occasionally our broadcasts are tied to a certain date or event on the calendar. For instance, I've always enjoyed running a piece each Christmas about the post office in Santa Claus, Indiana, that adds staff to handle the mountain of cards they receive for special holiday postmarks. Respectively, when late October rolls around, I'm always looking for a spooky tale appropriate for Halloween. I found one historic and haunting tale on a trip to the northeast.

In 1692 the witches and goblins of Halloween suddenly seemed to have human faces. They were the faces of residents in the small town of Salem, Massachusetts. Within the span of a few short months, what began as accusations against a few would grow to affect almost everyone in the area. By the end of that year, twenty people would be put to death for crimes they didn't commit.

It began in January of 1692, when some young girls in Salem started to exhibit strange behavior, including bouts of screaming, trances, and evil visions. Elizabeth Parris and Abigail Williams were two of the first girls to fall ill. Doctors were summoned to help cure the strange ailments, but no one could find a remedy. The odd behavior continued and citizens struggled to find answers. Soon leaders in the very religious community would determine that the girls were under the influence of Satan. They believed the girls had been put under a spell by witches living in the town of Salem.

There was intense pressure placed upon the young ladies to identify who had brought the evil upon them. Elizabeth Paris' father had a Carib Indian slave, Tituba. She was one of the first to be accused because she was known to tell stories of voodoo and witchcraft from her native Barbados.

Tituba seemed to be a logical scapegoat. She was an outsider and was already telling stories that ran counter to the faith of those in Salem. On March 1, Tituba confessed to practicing witchcraft and proclaimed that there were many in the town who shared her beliefs. Meanwhile, the afflicted girls also named Sarah Good and Sarah Osborne, two townswomen, as witches who had put a spell upon them.

During the month of March, several young girls would bring more accusations against the citizens of Salem, leveling the charge of practicing witchcraft. The accused were often, though not always, women who were poor or socially unacceptable in the community. By May 27, the governor of the colony convened a special court to hear the cases against the Salem witches. On June 10, Bridget Bishop would be the first to hang. Before being led to the gallows, she would state, "I am no witch. I am innocent. I know nothing of it."

Throughout the summer of 1692, more of Salem's citizens were put to death. Some of those led to the gallows were pious members of Salem. One such citizen, Rebecca Nurse, was accused by the girls of placing spells upon them. During the summer of 1692 the jury heard her case and voted her not guilty. When the result was read, the afflicted girls burst into another of their infamous fits, and the judge told the jury they should discuss the case further. The second time they voted Bishop guilty and she was hanged.

Finally, the accusations proved too much for most citizens to believe. How could so much evil be in one town? Almost two hundred people had been imprisoned, and two dogs had even been executed as accomplices to the witches! By October, twenty people had been executed for the crime of practicing witchcraft. Governor Phips was under pressure to do something about the abundance of accusations and executions taking place in Salem. Ironically, this made-for-Halloween story would be brought to a halt just two days before Halloween. On October 29, Governor Phips dissolved the court, although other cases were still pending. Soon the general court of the colony created the Superior Court to try those remaining cases. When those individuals were tried in May of 1693, no one was convicted.

In time, one of the little girls, Anne Putnam, asked for forgiveness. Twelve years after the trials, at the age of twenty-four, she confessed that she had lied. Others who had served on juries expressed remorse that they had believed the wild tales of witches flying on broomsticks.

The real heroes in this story are the people who were executed. If they had confessed to practicing witchcraft, their lives would most likely have been spared. That is what many of the accused did in fact do. However, a handful did not betray their faith. They would not confess to a crime they did not commit. They were the citizens who were put to death. The names of those who perished that summer are memorialized in Salem.

This sad affair gave rise to the term "witch hunt" and remains a lesson to us today. We cannot afford to make decisions based on rumor. Gossip serves no purpose except to hurt. In Salem, gossip led to death. There is also an important lesson to be learned about standing up for what you hold dearly. To the condemned, their faith and good names were something for which they would give their lives. History records many who have died for their faith, their countries, or their families. Their deaths serve to inspire many to hold fast to their causes. What cause do you hold dear? Do you hurt others through rumor and gossip? Everyone should heed the lessons learned in Salem during the summer of 1692.

Duck Parade
MEMPHIS, TENNESSEE

"Man's mind, stretched to a new idea,
never goes back to its original dimensions."

—OLIVER WENDELL HOLMES

You just never know who might step off the elevator when it stops at a floor. However, you usually expect it to be a person and not farm animals!

It all began at the historic Peabody hotel back in the early 1930s in Memphis, Tennessee. Hotel general manager Frank Schutt and a friend went on a hunting trip and Frank asked the hotel chef to pack a picnic basket for the two sportsmen. Along with the food in the basket, the chef included some Tennessee sipping whiskey. When the men returned to the hotel that evening, none of the food had been eaten, but not a drop of the whiskey remained.

Live duck decoys were legal at the time and as Schutt and his hunting partner stepped into the lobby that evening, they realized they needed a place to keep their ducks. The lobby fountain seemed the perfect spot.

Guests loved having real ducks in the fountain. In fact, the guests liked these ducks so much that they hoped they would remain in the fountain. That's just what happened. In 1940, Peabody bellman Edward Pembroke, a former circus animal trainer, became the hotel's first duck master. He taught the ducks to "march" across the lobby and into the lobby fountain. Pembroke held the title of duck master for over fifty years and today has a hotel suite named in his honor.

On this day I headed up to the rooftop duck palace with current duck master Kalyn Housdan. His job is to care for the ducks, clean their palace, and make sure they are healthy and happy. Most importantly, he teaches the ducks to march. New ducks arrive here every three months, and Kalyn must spend about two weeks working with the new recruits. He trains the five mallards from seven to nine in the morning on the roof of the Peabody. The early morning workout helps the ducks and their master avoid the crowds that head upstairs later in the day to see the ducks' accommodations.

As we headed to the Peabody Duck Palace, Kalyn unlocked the mansion and roused the five celebrities. From here it was only a short walk across the roof to a bank of elevators. Kalyn used a key to hold the car at the roof with the doors open. The ducks waddled into position. They gave an occasional "quack" and quickly made the confines smell like a stockyards.

I served as timekeeper. The ducks had to arrive in the lobby promptly at 11:00 A.M. and I was to let Kalyn know when it was exactly 10:59. At that point he used the elevator phone to call the lobby and let the staff know we were on our way. It was as if we were the Secret Service moving the president. Every move had to be precise if the day's duck parade was to come off without a hitch.

The staff at the Peabody knows to begin playing a tape of Sousa's "King Cotton" march exactly one minute after they receive Kalyn's call. We held the car for another twenty seconds before allowing the doors to close. It takes forty seconds to make a non-stop descent fourteen stories to the hotel lobby. Even though these ducks experience this every day, it was an anxious ride as they began to waddle to the front of the car and prepare for the doors to open.

As the elevator light indicated "L" we could hear Sousa's "King Cotton" begin to play. The doors opened to reveal a red carpet leading thirty feet to the center of the lobby and the fountain. Hundreds of guests and visitors lined the walkway, snapping pictures as if we were actors heading into the Oscars.

The duck march takes only a minute. As the ducks began their daily six-hour swim, spectators continued to jockey for the best angle around the fountain. For me, this was the closest I will ever come to stardom. No doubt, hundreds of pictures were developed of the ducks making their way from the elevator to the fountain. In each picture, behind the ducks, each tourist saw me and undoubtedly asked, "Who is that moron chasing the ducks with a microphone?"

It's not every day you ride an elevator with five mallards and a duck master. Not only is the Peabody a luxurious and historic hotel, it is enhanced by five mallards who bring in hundreds of guests and tourists each day. It's a unique niche that makes this place special. Each of us should consider our own niche that turns ordinary to extraordinary.

The Green File

JEFFERSON CITY, MISSOURI

> *"Kind words can be short and easy to speak,
> but their echoes are truly endless."*
>
> — MOTHER TERESA

The phone number had been on the wall for over two years. During that time, other numbers had come and gone. Each was important for a time as it related to a story that one of the news network's reporters was covering. What was odd was that only one number, the number for a Super 8 motel, had never been erased. I finally asked the logical question: "What is that phone number for?" At that point, an intriguing story began to unfold about one of the most difficult news reports our radio network covers.

I have never been a fulltime news reporter. However, my work puts me in touch with many broadcasters, including the crew at the Missouri Net, the Show-Me state's radio news network. I will occasionally file a report for their newscasts and am very familiar with their work. When I'm in the office, my desk at the Brownfield Radio Network sits only a few feet from their news workroom. I know all of the reporters and we help each other out from time to time, sharing facts about a story we think might be helpful to one of our fellow broadcasters. So it wasn't unusual for me to ask my friend and fellow broadcaster, Brent Martin, what that phone number was all about.

He seemed surprised by my question. "You don't know what that number is for?" he asked in return.

I couldn't imagine what was so important about a Super 8 motel. I had never heard any mention of this lodging in any news broadcast for the past three years and I knew they weren't a sponsor of the news either. Still, Brent seemed puzzled that I could have been around the newsroom that long and not have figured out why a reporter might need that number.

He motioned for me to come over to a filing cabinet and he pulled open the drawer. It was full of green file folders. He reached down and opened one of the files. The contents of that folder began to explain the reason that phone number remained on the wall every day of the year.

Inside every one of those files was a picture of a man or woman who was to be recognized at the news event held near the Super 8. Inside was a list of accomplishments, important details explaining the feats each person had attained to earn them their reward. Important dates were listed that would be of benefit to the network's reporters. In fact, as I scanned the data, I recognized names and dates from several past news stories.

Brent explained that before the event, the reporter who would cover it needed to call the motel phone number listed on the wall in order to make a reservation. A long drive from home, it was always late when the news conference was completed. This was the only regularly occurring story that required an overnight stay.

Every reporter at the network knows that there is only one story that requires a hotel stay at the Super 8 in Potosi, Missouri. The event to be covered takes place at 12:01 A.M. That's when a man's or woman's list of "accomplishments" will lead him or her to die by lethal injection.

Every time a network reporter goes to the Super 8 motel in Potosi, they cover the same event. You can be assured that they are given a green file folder late in the evening and then enter a room that is often eerily silent.

To this day, that phone number is still on the wall. It is a haunting reminder of the breadth of the stories the network covers. Our radio network and our reporters have interviewed great political and civic leaders. We've interviewed Emmy and Grammy winners, sports stars, and other celebrities. I often ask myself, "How does one person become a popular and well-known celebrity while another is executed in Potosi?"

Time and time again we hear about students graduating high school or college, or an adult winning a big award, and they will say something like, "If it wasn't for my teacher back in the second grade I wouldn't be here today." Often the person who made a difference in the award winner's life was someone who influenced them at a very early age.

Each one of us can probably remember several times when a parent, grandparent, friend, or teacher said something to us that really gave us a lift when we needed it the most. They may never have realized that what they said or did impacted us so much, yet it did make a big difference. I know that I can look back on several such instances in my own life.

We may never know the difference positive words or caring actions can make in a person's life. No, I cannot say that a few positive words early in life would have kept every man and women out of the penitentiary in Potosi. Each of us ultimately has to take responsibility for our own actions. However, we should never underestimate the difference caring people can make in the world.

So many people have related to me how just a few positive words or a caring action turned their lives around. They will tell me about that special person who helped them reach success. Maybe it's just taking an extra moment to do something nice for a stranger, or making a special effort to give someone a lift when they're feeling low. Each of us should look for ways to make that difference in the lives of others.

The need for that phone number at the Super 8 will probably never go away, but each of us has the ability to help others find purpose and success in life. It is my hope that each of us will apply ourselves to that task.

Digging Deep

GREENSBURG, KANSAS

"A wise man will make more opportunities than he finds."

—FRANCIS BACON

It may not be Disney World, but it's the biggest tourist attraction along Highway 54 west of Wichita, Kansas. Ironically, it was never designed to lure one single visitor to town, yet it has now drawn over three million people here to see it. Even more ironically, the thing it was supposed to lure to town never arrived.

It all began around 1887 as railroads were laying tracks across the high plains. As those lines crossed the nation, many communities worked hard to lure the rail lines to pass through their towns. Railroads often meant the difference between life and death for these small towns.

Greensburg, Kansas, was one such place. In 1887, in an effort to lure a rail line near, Greensburg wanted to stand out. They knew there needed to be something special about this town in order for the railroad to choose to come here instead of somewhere else. Their answer was to begin digging a giant well that could service both the new rail line and the growing town. The well would not only provide water for the townspeople, steam locomotives could also use the resource to recharge their tanks.

The project was immense, with the dig taking about one year. Dirt from the well was loaded on wagons and hauled toward the

Medicine River, twelve miles from town. As the wagons made the trip, slats in the wagon box were opened, allowing the dirt to gradually fall out the bottom of the box. That dirt helped fill the wagon ruts left from the many trips back and forth to the river. When the wagon reached the end of the trail, large stones were loaded from the stream bed for use in the well lining. The routine continued for weeks with the wagons carrying soil out and stone back, all while a giant hole was being dug further into the earth.

At one point a mule was even lowered to the bottom of the well to assist with the final portion of the dig. Any reference to the mule (who loved to kick) was almost always preceded with the word "damn." Picks, shovels, barrels, and mules eventually helped dig a well 32 feet wide and 109 feet deep. It remains the deepest hand dug well in the world.

The town of Greensburg was ready to cash in on the rail line that was sure to pass through town. They now stood out when compared to the competition. They had the deepest hand dug well and enough water to supply the locomotives that would pass through. There was only one problem. By 1888, the Santa Fe railroad had decided not to run a line through Greensburg after all. Greensburg now had the largest hand dug well and no railroad to show for it.

There was no need to let the well and the water go to waste, so Greensburg began using the well to supply its citizens with water. Still, having the deepest hand dug well in the world was very small consolation. What good was the distinction? Not only that, by 1930, the water in the well was determined to be unfit to drink. Now Greensburg had a giant hole that served no purpose at all.

Most cities would have taken the next logical step. They would have swallowed their defeat and simply filled in the large hole. Not Greensburg. Sure, they had lost the railroad almost half a century earlier. But now was the time the well could pay even bigger dividends.

Instead of calling in bulldozers to finish off the relic, townspeople called in construction crews to build a set of stairs to the bottom of the well.

Soon signs were placed along major highways in Kansas urging travelers to descend into the world's deepest hand dug well. No longer was this a giant mistake. This was THE deepest hand dug well and YOU could not only see it, YOU could go to the bottom of it! So who would drive out of their way to come to Greensburg to see a well? To this date, over three million visitors have descended those stairs, each paying a small fee to make the trip.

It's a classic example of turning problems into solutions. In the face of utter defeat, leaders often turn failure into victory. They choose to look at opportunities instead of complaining about their misfortunes. A well once dug to attract a railroad now draws tourists from every state in the nation and visitors from around the world. No doubt, the deepest hand dug well earns far more tourist dollars than it ever would have generated in rail income.

How do we treat our defeats? Do we see them as opportunities to achieve in new ways? This was a lesson I learned when I descended the steps of the world's deepest hand dug well . . . a truly unique tourist attraction.

Days Once Ended at Sunset
West Orange, New Jersey

"Everybody is ignorant, only on different subjects."

—Will Rogers

Today the laboratories and factories are quiet, except for the foot traffic of tourists who have found their way off Interstate 280 and have driven a couple of miles to get here. Once, this complex was the site of some of the greatest minds in the world, each dedicated to helping others develop inventions that would change the way people worked and lived. Today, the area stands as a silent reminder of the impact one person can have on the lives of others.

Ironically, the man behind it all had but a few months of formal education. Born in Milan, Ohio, the boy called "Al" would receive much of his schooling at home with his mother serving as teacher. But there was something special about that boy . . . a boy the world would come to know as Thomas Edison.

At the age of twelve, young Edison was selling newspapers and candy on the Grand Trunk Railroad. He even began printing his own paper onboard the train and conducted scientific experiments in a boxcar in his spare time.

At the age of fifteen a heroic deed would open the doors of technology to him. He noticed a three-year-old child playing on the railroad tracks. When Thomas spotted the child he also noticed a boxcar rolling toward the toddler. Edison ran across the tracks and rescued the child from being hit. The grateful father, J. U. MacKenzie, offered to teach him telegraphy as a reward.

Thomas Edison worked as a railroad telegrapher for the next four years, moving to several different cities in the process. During that time, his mind began to dream of ways to build new machines that would change life for the better. In 1869 Edison patented his first invention, a vote recorder. Politicians, however, were leery of the machine, believing it would somehow miscount votes in favor of their opponents, and the new device was not used.

With his background in telegraphy, Edison formed several partnerships and companies devoted to making improvements to the telegraph. In 1871 he married a former employee, Mary Stillwell. He taught her Morse code and the two were known to tap messages to one another on the backs of their hands. In fact, Edison's marriage proposal came in the form of one of those messages tapped on his bride's hand. He wrote in his diary, "The word 'yes' is an easy one to send by telegraph signal, and she sent it."

The simple story of his marriage proposal reflected the way Edison often looked at life. His mind was constantly looking at ways to turn the ordinary into the extraordinary. Ironically, even such little "innovations" like tapping his marriage proposal would change life for the better. Late in life, when Edison had grown nearly deaf, he had great difficulty hearing the dialogue of movies (one of his very own inventions). His wife would hold his hand and tap out the words so he could follow the story line.

Countless biographers have outlined the many innovations Edison made. I won't attempt to list them all here, but Edison's goal was to turn out a minor invention every ten days and a big one every six months. In the end, that attitude led him to file 1,093 patents.

At a press conference late in life he was asked what was the greatest invention ever made. That's quite a question to be answered by the prime inventor himself! What would he say? Would he list one of his own inventions? Would he choose a simple invention from centuries ago?

He simply replied, "The mind of a child."

Edison never lost that childlike curiosity that led him to experiment and invent. He also surrounded his curiosity with the knowledge to turn dreams into realities. In fact, if you tour Edison's office, you will find it is like none other. His desk sits in the middle of a large, three-story-tall room. The middle of the room is open all the way to the ceiling, giving the office the look of a modern day atrium. However, the perimeter of the room, on all three levels, is lined with rows and rows of books. Small sets of stairs allow access to the floors and books. Edison surrounded himself with knowledgeable people and important information. He didn't have all of the answers, but he placed himself in a position to succeed.

Once upon a time, people's days ended with the setting of the sun. Edison's light bulb changed that. Curiosity and knowledge were never lost in his life. Those qualities helped change the world. Finding those qualities in our own lives can lead to a new perspective on life that we have never before known.

Cyberspace Congregation

CARMEL, CALIFORNIA

"Behold, I stand at the door, and knock; if any man hear my voice, and opens the door, I will come in to him, and will sup with him, and he with me."

—REVELATION 3:20

It was a beautiful sunny day when I drove up the winding lane to the Pacific Meadows Retirement Community in Carmel, California. The hilltop offered a sweeping view of the Pacific Ocean and the rolling countryside. It was the type of scene you see on the front of a postcard.

I wheeled into the parking lot and spotted an older gentlemen waving to me from a second story deck. It had to be Pastor Boyd. I had never met him before, but he was there to wave to me, letting me know I was in the right place.

I had heard a lot about the pastor's work, but I just had to go visit with him in person. At the age of eighty-five he was still doing the Lord's work, reaching people all across the nation and around the world.

For most of his adult life, Gerald Boyd had served as a pastor at three different churches. Although he had retired from full-time ministry, he still looked for ways to serve God. One of those ways was by teaching an evening Bible study. It was during one of those classes one night that a young businessman came to him with a most interesting proposal. Gerald related, "He came to me after class and said, 'Pastor, how would you like to be my missionary on the Internet?' and I thought, 'Well that sounds interesting.'"

Keep in mind, Gerald was eighty years old at the time. He did have a computer, but he was far from computer literate. "I bought a laptop computer to keep my mind active so I wouldn't get Alzheimer's," he joked. However, his laptop went mostly unused. He was not a computer user and didn't really see any need for it in his retirement.

Gerald was at least interested in learning about computers and the Internet, so he took the man up on the offer to surf the net and see how he might use it to minister to people in cyberspace. The demonstration was like giving a new toy to a child. Gerald was hooked! He learned how to talk to people in chat rooms and he began answering their questions about faith. He listened to their struggles and gave them suggestions on how to improve their situations.

"When I first started I was so excited to have this opportunity, I didn't want to stop to eat or go to sleep." In fact, his wife had to remind him to come to the dinner table. His businessman friend helped him set up a website at www.amazinggrace.com. Pastor Boyd also began to type and save several short messages on his computer. These messages helped answer common questions people seemed to have for him in the chat rooms. He also made the messages available on his website.

Those short messages are an important part of his ministry. When Gerald is talking with folks in a chat room, he can save a lot of time by simply inserting a few lines from a pre-typed message to help answer their questions. When on-line, Gerald goes by the name "GBREV320." The name stands for Revelation 3:20 in the Bible, the invitation of Christ to all who hear. There are plenty of people who visit with the pastor online. Often they will ask "GBREV320" his opinion on issues in their lives. Those conversations may continue over the course of a few days, weeks, or even months. These dialogues often change lives.

"This has fulfilled my fondest dreams," Gerald told me. "If a person is interested in souls, the Internet is loaded. It actually drives me night and day to communicate." Gerald now often spends up to six hours per day at his keyboard. He visits chat rooms that deal with Christian topics. Even though the title "Christian" may be on the chat room, a lot of people will come to such cyber rooms to find answers to their problems. On the other hand, others arrive in the chat room to "trash" the importance of faith in a person's life. So, Gerald finds plenty of people to encourage and inspire.

Ironically, many of this retired pastor's conversations are with teenagers. Younger people spend more time on-line and they are dealing with many difficult decisions. Gerald shared with me some of the e-mails he has received. The e-letters bring you to tears, as many teens share stories of brokenness and despair and are simply looking for answers to overwhelming questions.

Often, these teens will have no idea how old Gerald actually is, though sometimes the topic does come up. "They are amazed," he told me. "They say, 'Are you really *eighty-five?*' They are surprised that I type as well as I do. I tell them that God gave me a good mind, nimble fingers, and no arthritis!"

While Gerald helps individuals find support in their local communities, sometimes those who find him on the net feel more comfortable continuing to "talk" to him. "I try to encourage them to counsel with their own pastor, but sometimes they feel too intimidated and they can talk to you over the Internet because they don't see you, and you're ready to give them an answer from the Word."

The Internet has served as a wonderful way for this retired pastor to continue to minister and counsel others, even students who might be seventy years younger than him. Before I departed, Gerald asked if I would have time for a short prayer. It was a nice conclusion to our visit. We prayed that his ministry would continue to change lives, and I prayed that telling this story might help readers with some of their difficulties.

"Whatever your situation is, God changes lives and that's His mission. Our ministry's goal is to present to you the opportunity to know Christ who is able to change you, resolve your problems, and to give you a peace you've never known before." It's an important message for all to ponder.

Tastes Like Chicken
CORBIN, KENTUCKY

*"Example is the school of mankind,
and they will learn at no other."*

—EDMUND BURKE

I t all began in a little gas station on the old Dixie Highway in Corbin, Kentucky. A middle-aged man by the name of Harlan was trying to make ends meet by selling gas and running a motel and small restaurant. Although he would eventually become a very successful businessman later in life, times in the early 1930s were tough. Not only was money tight due to the Depression, a fire swept through his buildings, destroying almost everything.

The fire was a setback, but also served as an opportunity for Harlan to reconsider his business plan. After careful thought, he decided not to reopen the restaurant and instead chose to focus on building a great motel and operating his small station. If Harlan Sanders had stuck with that decision, one of the world's great fast-food retailers would not be here today.

Or course, the restaurant did get rebuilt, on the advice of a friend. Sanders recalled that the friend said to him, "You can sleep a man only once in a day, but you can feed him three times." The opportunity to make more money by serving meals appealed to Harlan and so the café reopened as well.

The "Colonel" as he was known (Governor Ruby Laffoon made him a Kentucky colonel in 1935) was forty years old before he began to experiment with the unique blend of herbs and spices that would make his chicken famous. The original café really wasn't a café at all. Travelers would pull up a seat around the dinner table in his gas station, and he could only seat six people at a time. By 1937, his reputation as a good cook meant that the operation had to expand. The restaurant moved across the street and seating capacity increased from six to nearly 150.

In the early 1950s Interstate 75 drew traffic away from the old Dixie Highway and business began to dwindle. Sanders had relied upon the steady flow of traffic up and down the major north-south thoroughfare. With the traffic and much of his business gone, he sold his restaurant and at the age of sixty-five hit the road to begin franchising. The sale of the business was barely enough to pay his bills, and he was forced to live off his monthly Social Security check of $105.

Sanders was able to convince restaurant owners to use his chicken frying method and to become franchisees. He steadily gained more and more business and by 1964, Sanders sold his interest in the company for two million dollars. There were over six hundred outlets at that time. Today, that number tops ten thousand worldwide.

Sanders was a stickler for frying chicken the right way. It's said that if he visited a franchise that was not performing up to par, he might take away its pressure cookers and paint over its signs. Some of those who knew Sanders here in Corbin say that he could be a demanding boss, yet he was just making sure things were done the right way.

The original restaurant is still open for business, though a modern retail outlet has been attached to the older building and kitchen where Sanders perfected his work. It makes for a merger of the old and new way Sanders' customers are served.

In spite of the success of his chicken, Harlan Sanders' greatest marketing move may have come in the motel business, and it can still be seen in Corbin at the original restaurant today. When fried chicken sales at his small café were booming, he built a replica motel room inside his restaurant. Every lady who went to the restroom had to pass by that model hotel room, and consequently his motel business boomed as well. Finicky ladies saw the cleanliness of the replica room and decided the place would be fit for their families to spend the night. Harlan Sanders didn't "tell them," he "showed them." It was exactly the same process he used to sell franchises as he traveled the nation frying his chicken for potential franchisees. It's an important lesson about how we win the hearts, minds, and stomachs of others. Don't just tell them about it. *Show* them.

Rental Car Thief

PEORIA, ILLINOIS

"When I am employed in serving others I do not look upon myself as conferring favors but paying debts."

— BENJAMIN FRANKLIN

By the time I landed at the Peoria airport it was already 2:45 A.M. Violent thunderstorms had prevented our small turboprop from leaving Minneapolis for over five hours. Now, in the early hours of the morning, the skies had cleared to reveal a beautiful star-scape across the dark midwestern sky.

Realizing that my plane would be arriving very late, I found the number for the rental car counter in Peoria and, before even taking off from Minneapolis, I gave them a call to let them know I still intended to pick up my rental car when my plane landed. The young lady on the phone said that if I did not arrive before midnight, she would leave her phone number on the rental counter so I could call her. She said it wouldn't be a problem for her to drive back to the airport since she lived only five minutes from there.

I finally landed in Peoria. I got my luggage and headed over to the rental car counter. It was almost 3:00 A.M. and the rental car area was deserted. No problem. I knew the phone number would be waiting there for me. Problem. After much searching, I could not find a phone number anywhere. The airport was deserted. I was alone.

At this point I had been awake for twenty-two straight hours and I still had a two-hour drive ahead of me in order to make my 8:00 A.M. appointment. Either I was going to have to sleep in the airport until 6:00 A.M. when someone would return (at least that's what the car company's sign stated), or I was going to have to find another way out of there.

It's funny what a man will resort to when he has been deserted at the Peoria airport at 3:00 A.M. I took a look around to make sure no one was watching and then dove over the rental car counter. I was determined not to come out of there until I had found a set of keys to a rental car. Would it really be stealing a car if I "found" a set of keys and had already rented a car from this company? I really didn't care. I figured I would have the car back to them before the state patrol would find me. At least, that's how I rationalized pilfering the car counter.

After a few minutes rummaging through the unlocked drawers, I uncovered a small, worn piece of paper with a few first names and phone numbers on it. Above the rental car counter I had found a sign that stated "John" was the manager of the facility. The phone list had a "John" on it. I didn't know who "John" was, but he was about to get a call from me at 3:30 A.M. Besides, the car keys were in a locked drawer and I didn't have a crowbar with me.

After several rings someone answered. It was obvious this man had been enjoying a good night's rest before my call. He was in fact the manager! Not only that, once I explained my situation, he thanked me for giving him a call. He said he would be dressed and there within ten minutes.

Just before 4:00 A.M. I drove out of Peoria with my rental car. "John" apologized for his employee who had left me stranded. He thanked me for taking the time to give him a call and even gave me the biggest car on the lot.

Twelve hours later I returned to the Peoria airport. My radio interview and speaking engagement for the day were complete and I had even managed to get two hours of sleep during the day. My plane pulled up to the gate a few minutes before our scheduled departure time. At small airports such as this, it is not unusual for the gate agents to leave the counter and unload the plane. All but two of the sixteen scheduled passengers had already checked in.

Suddenly, the fourteen of us in the boarding lounge heard someone shouting. A rather large, middle-aged lady loaded down with luggage was waddling toward our gate, the only gate at this end of the airport. She looked behind her and shouted to her husband to hurry up. I would have rather tried to stop a charging Brahma bull than stand in the way of this lady. She was mad and she was in a hurry. She was convinced that she had missed her flight . . . the same flight the other fourteen of us were still waiting to board.

Soon she barreled by us, not even noticing that we were the passengers who would also be on her flight. She was convinced that the plane sitting outside the large pane of glass was loaded and ready for take-off. No gate agents were at the counter. They were loading luggage on the plane.

In a desperate attempt to board the plane, she began banging her fists on the locked door that led to the tarmac. She shouted at the agents beyond the pane of glass (the fact that the propellers were turning and the agents were wearing earplugs didn't seem to diminish her efforts).

A helpful fellow passenger, like myself, would have gladly gone over to her and told her there was no reason to worry. But after spending thirty-four of the last thirty-six hours awake, I wasn't about to walk over there. This was some real entertainment! Besides, after seeing the way she yelled at her husband and the gate agents (who couldn't hear her), her bad attitude really made me not want to help her.

After five minutes of banging on the windows and fruitless yelling at the agents loading the luggage on the plane, the lady finally saw an agent heading toward the door. I don't think she ever noticed the other fourteen of us patiently sitting and waiting to board. The agent was barely able to grab her ticket before she ran out to the plane that she believed was ready to take off.

I later learned that the agents had in fact seen her banging on the windows. However, she had been verbally abusive to one of their fellow agents back at the main ticket counter. They weren't about to do anything to help this rude lady. It turned out they were having as much fun watching the entire scene as those of us in the boarding area.

My twelve hours at the Peoria airport taught me some important lessons about dealing with people. You can be guaranteed that if I ever need to fly to Peoria again, I will be renting a car from "John's" company. The time he took to help me in the wee hours of the morning really meant a lot.

I also saw what happens when you treat people poorly and have a bad attitude. They won't budge one inch to come to your aid. The poor lady at the Peoria airport probably thought that people were "out to get her." However, a little patience and kindness would have brought gate agents and passengers to her aid. Instead, she became our in-flight entertainment.

It's all about how we treat others and it means a lot . . . even outside the Greater Peoria Airport.

Coffee and Contras

Boston, Massachusetts, and Esteli, Nicaragua

*"Keep your face to the sunshine
and you cannot see the shadows."*

—Helen Keller

Many people would say that Santiago doesn't have much in life. He and his family are coffee farmers in northern Nicaragua. Life in this part of the country can be much like the landscape itself . . . rough, rocky, an uphill climb. Farm families survive by simply growing an acre or two of shade grown coffee (coffee that grows in the shade of taller hillside trees) and raising a few chickens or hogs. This is a place that knows all too well the struggles of a developing nation.

In 1936, General Anastasio Somoza led a takeover of the Nicaraguan government and from 1937 to 1979, members of the Somoza family ruled the nation. It was a time of unrest, with many in this nation hoping to someday topple Somoza's regime and return control to the citizens.

In the 1970s more organized opposition to the Somoza government arose in the form of the Sandinista National Liberation Front, often referred to as the Sandinistas for short. The Sandinistas are named after Augusto Cesar Sandino, a popular Nicaraguan freedom fighter who was executed by Anastasio Somoza in 1934. In fact,

Sandino's picture appears throughout the country, a symbol of heroism and freedom to many.

The Sandinistas did obtain control of the government in 1979, but there was still political unrest in the country. The United States charged that Nicaragua was providing weapons to rebel groups in other Central American nations. By 1981, former members of Samoza's army began launching attacks from northern neighbor Honduras, trying to seize the reigns of government once again. Somoza's old forces were referred to as the Contras and received the backing of the U.S.

Those raids across the border of Honduras and Nicaragua placed war all around Santiago's home. Almost twenty years later, northern Nicaragua still feels the effects of the civil war. Many families live in poverty. Some buildings in Esteli still show the scars of bullets. The coffee cooperative was one of the buildings targeted by the Contras. Locals say they made it a target because it was a place where farmers banded together to sell their crops. The Contras hoped to destroy those symbols of unity and destroy the morale of the area farmers.

Santiago's home was a very simple structure. It had three rooms with a small lean-to kitchen attached to one wall. A few chickens and one pig roamed inside a split-rail pen just a few feet from the front door. On the wall of the largest room was a picture of Santiago's son in military fatigues (he was killed by the Contras). Next to it was a picture of the Virgin Mary.

In the late 1990s, an American-based group that promotes the fair trade of coffee flew Santiago to the U.S. to speak of the plight of Central America's coffee farmers. It was the first time that Santiago had taken a hot shower in his life. His home had electricity, but no running water. His family simply did without many of the simple conveniences American households take for granted.

My journey to cover this story began in Boston with an organization named OxFam America. This non-profit anti-hunger and poverty group assists with many projects around the world, and the fair trade coffee campaign is one of their important initiatives. I made the journey to Santiago's home as a journalist covering the plight of these Nicaraguan coffee farmers. I had joined a small group of coffee retailers who had come to Central America to learn more about this same story as well. On the winding gravel road that passes Santiago's home, a mule train packed bags of coffee toward town. The harvest and processing of the coffee beans is still almost entirely done by hand. Automation is absent. If Santiago's home and farm were in the U.S., they would be a part of a historical site. Here, the scene is not a history field trip; it is reality.

On this day, these U.S. coffee company representatives made a special trip to see his farm. They originally met him when he traveled to California, and they now had the opportunity to actually see his farm in Nicaragua. Santiago and some of his neighbor farmers even brought out their musical instruments and put on a concert for their visitors. It was a wonderful time for everyone with young and old, Americans and Nicaraguans, taking time to dance to songs these farmers had written. The melodies drifted through the hills and soon a group of farm families had walked to the homestead to join in the event.

As the Americans prepared to leave, Santiago wanted to share one final message. Through an interpreter he thanked the group for coming to visit. He thanked them for buying his coffee. It was his final statement that will be remembered by that group for a very long time. He said, "I enjoyed meeting you in America. Maybe someday I will get to return and visit you again. You have to return today to your homes, and your jobs in the big city. I get to stay here to work with my hands in the coffee fields. I get to enjoy the beautiful sunshine and the wonderful music of my neighbors. I have my family to work with me. I am the lucky one."

Santiago has experienced more war than peace in his life. He has taken one hot shower. He may never own an automobile. A three-room home, a mule, and some chickens may be the most wealth he will ever know. Yet Santiago feels he is the lucky one. Santiago appreciates what he has . . . his family, his neighbors, the beautiful weather, and his physical ability to work in the fields.

We often spend too much time looking at what we don't have in life. It's certainly fine to dream, plan, and achieve, but do we overlook the precious things that are all around us? Too many people live sad and depressed lives because they never take time to look at what they do have. Few Americans will probably ever know what it is like to live in a home with dirt floors and the threat of war all around them. For that, take time to say thanks.

Cereal City
BATTLE CREEK, MICHIGAN

"Associate yourself with men of good quality if you esteem your own reputation; for 'tis better to be alone than in bad company."

—GEORGE WASHINGTON

If you've looked at the back of just about any cereal box, you've probably seen the name of this city. In fact, so much cereal is made here, it's often referred to as the "Cereal City." It's an interesting story that has as its roots the old Battle Creek Sanitarium and the Seventh-Day Adventist Church.

In 1860, church members in Battle Creek, Michigan, chose the name Seventh Day Adventist for their congregation. Five years earlier, the church had established a print house to publish religious literature here. James and Ellen G. White were early leaders in the Adventist movement and they helped oversee the printery. A boy who set type at the print house caught the eye of the founders. His name was John Harvey Kellogg. The Whites recognized the boy's potential and helped him further his education by helping pay his way to school to become a doctor.

Dr. Kellogg and his brother W. K. lived not only a religious life, they adopted a vegetarian lifestyle in accordance with church rules. Healthy lifestyles were very important to church members, and in 1866 the Western Health Reform Institute (later renamed the Battle Creek Sanitarium or "San") was established in Battle Creek. Ellen White oversaw the work of the institute for its first ten years before Dr. Kellogg became its director, a position he held for over sixty years.

The Kelloggs were constantly searching for ways to improve the diets of patients at the sanitarium. Because Seventh Day Adventists are vegetarians, the Kelloggs were searching for meat substitutes to put on the dinner table. At one point, Dr. Kellogg experimented with nut products as a solution, even publishing a paper titled "Nuts May Save the Race." Some historians even credit Kellogg with inventing peanut butter.

Other food research dealt with boiling grains, especially wheat. One day in 1894, a pot of boiled wheat was accidentally left to stand when the Kelloggs were suddenly called away to tend to other business. When W. K. Kellogg returned, he found the wheat had become tempered. He rolled the tempered wheat and discovered that it made large thin flakes. Up until this point, any attempts to roll the grains had resulted in a paste that stuck to the rollers. With the accidental discovery of tempering grain, flakes could now be made. The process was used to make the first corn flakes.

The Battle Creek Sanitarium was the equivalent of today's health resort. People from across the country would come here to regain their health from a myriad of ailments. The Kellogg brothers did much more than just discover and manufacture cereal. Dr. Kellogg developed many "cures" that were implemented at the sanitarium. In fact, I once sat in a vibrating chair that Dr. Kellogg invented. It was supposed to help you better digest your food. I found it just gave me a headache!

Over a century later, Duff Stoltz, maintenance manager at Cereal City USA, helped retell the story to me. On this snowy day, I found him in the parking lot clearing snow. Duff knows his history, a wealth of facts about the cereal story, and its links to Battle Creek and the Adventist Church.

Duff related that when the Kelloggs began serving their new flaked grain at the Sanitarium, patients wanted to be able to purchase the same food when they returned to their homes. Soon a mail order business developed and the Kelloggs found themselves manufacturing cereal for consumers far from Battle Creek.

In 1891, C. W. Post came to the San as a patient. He spent nine months at the institute and learned all he could about the diet and health regime of Dr. Kellogg. Although he claimed he was not healed of the upset stomach for which he sought a cure, he did leave the San inspired to develop his own health foods. By 1895 he had developed Postum, a coffee substitute. In 1897 Grape Nuts would hit the market, followed by Elijah's Manna in 1904, later renamed Post Toasties. Post made unusual medical claims about his products, even promoting Grape Nuts as a cure for consumption, malaria, and loose teeth!

At the beginning of the twentieth century, several cereal companies were entering the market, trying to capture a piece of the new food niche. Other cereal companies that didn't have a factory in Battle Creek opened offices here anyway so they could legitimately put the town of Battle Creek on their boxes. This city had built a reputation as the "Health City" and everyone wanted to be associated with it.

As Duff and I looked through his collection of old cereal posters and memorabilia, he related that about one hundred cereal manufacturers have called Battle Creek their home. Over time, many of those companies have merged or gone out of business. However, three major cereal companies remain and they produce the vast majority of the cereals on the market.

Despite the success of the Kellogg Company today, Dr. Kellogg's company was floundering at the beginning of the twentieth century. While he was interested in developing new health remedies, he was not a businessman. Meanwhile, his brother W. K. convinced him that a new company should be formed to manufacture corn flakes. The Battle Creek Toasted Corn Flake Company was formed in 1906 and W. K. was placed in charge, although Dr. Kellogg owned a majority of the stock in the company. Dr. Kellogg distributed most of his stock to other doctors at the San.

Still, W. K. was not happy with the direction of the company. He wanted ownership control in addition to his directorship. When Dr.

Kellogg left for a trip to Europe, W. K. went to the doctors at the San and bought the stock given to them by Dr. Kellogg. This move gave W. K. majority control of the cereal manufacturer. W. K. eventually changed the company's name to the Kellogg Company and put his own signature on the box. From that point on, business soared and the Kellogg name became a mainstay in the cereal business.

Although many cereals still tout health benefits just as they did in the early 1900s, most companies have added colorful, sugary additions to their line-up. Duff brags that Battle Creek's air pollution is actually healthful since so many cereal fumes are blowing in the breeze. However, he does smile and admit that on the days they make Fruity Pebbles at Post and Fruit Loops at Kellogg's there may be too much sugar in the air! The sweet smell of cereal actually serves as a weather barometer for Duff. When he smells cereal in the west end of town that means a front is nearing and that rain or snow is likely on the way.

Battle Creek developed a solid reputation for helping people regain their health and for feeding them food that would keep them feeling great. Certainly, some of Dr. Kellogg's ideas were "interesting" to say the least, and the claims of some cereal companies probably stretched the truth. However, the reputation of the Cereal City was something every cereal manufacturer wanted to include in their story. Placing the name "Battle Creek" on the box was worth a lot to the consumer.

Understanding the power of a great reputation is an important lesson to each of us. Reputations are not built overnight, but instead are formed through years of trust. Each of us should take account of what reputation we build for ourselves. A great reputation is what began a cereal revolution in Battle Creek. A great reputation should be a must in our own lives as well.

Can I Take My Lawnmower on the Plane?

ATLANTA, GEORGIA

"Remember that a person's name is to that person the sweetest and most important sound in any language."

—DALE CARNEGIE

I t's one of the world's great aviation mysteries. Expeditions have spent thousands of hours searching for Amelia Earhart's plane. They have studied the strange disappearance of aircraft in the Bermuda Triangle. But nothing may be as difficult to explain as what happens to my luggage when it disappears down the baggage belt behind the check-in counter at the airport. I found the answer underneath Atlanta's Hartsfield International Airport.

I went to Atlanta and met Ron, who has worked in the baggage office at Delta Airlines for over three decades. He says bags used to just come down a metal chute to be sorted by hand. Today, optical scanners read bar codes on bag tags and automatically sort the luggage to "piers." It takes about eight minutes for luggage to go from the ticket counter to these piers. From there it may take another three to eight minutes for the bags to be loaded onto luggage carts and hauled to the appropriate plane. It all depends on how far away the plane is located from the sorting area.

At the beginning of 2001, Delta airlines handled 700,000 pieces of luggage every month in Atlanta. When you visit with the skycaps and baggage handlers who sort and load that massive amount of luggage, you begin to hear some very amazing stories. Probably the most interesting stories are the variety of things that people have tried to check onto an airplane.

For instance, did you know that you can claim a lawnmower as part of your checked baggage? That's exactly what one man did. His push mower was part of his luggage for the trip (no word on exactly why this mower had to do the trimming at his new destination). As long as the mower is in a box and it weighs under the weight limit (currently seventy pounds), it can be a part of your checked luggage.

Plenty of pets make the trip every year. Ron and his crew have seen a zoo-like variety of animals from dogs and cats to snakes and exotic birds. During his three decades sorting luggage, Ron has seen just about everything. So, I asked the logical question: "Exactly what is the strangest item you've put on a plane in the last thirty years?"

Ron answered, "One day I was sorting luggage and I heard a big crash on the belt behind me. I turned around to see what had come down the chute and there was a large electric welder. That's the weirdest thing I've seen."

Another day about thirty years ago stands out in Ron's mind as well. He was in the belly of a plane loading luggage. There was a downpour and the bags were wet. Just when he thought the monsoon was at its worst, a canoe came up the belt and into the plane. He laughed and said, "I thought it was a sign the airport had flooded."

Today Ron's job is to reunite bags with their owners. If passengers are rerouted or if a bag happens to miss a flight, he must find the bag, retag it, and get it to the right airport as quickly as possible. He says only ten to twenty bags per shift need his specialized attention. The most frustrating part of the job is when passengers don't put any identification on their luggage. Occasionally the airport bag tags come off the luggage. If there isn't identification on the bag, the situation can become a real mystery.

Have you ever thought about the power of a name? To Ron, a simple name represents the power to get luggage where it needs to be. But, names can do much more than just get luggage where it needs to be.

When I was eighteen years old, I had the fortune to be a part of a leadership training class taught by former Dale Carnegie instructor John Moats. It was a part of training for all newly elected state FFA officers. I devoured every shred of information that he shared with us during our three-day training course. His tips on working effectively with others and his keys to better speaking are still the basis for what I do today.

However, it was a trip to McDonald's that convinced me of this man's influence on others and he demonstrated it with a tool available to every single one of us. I was standing with him in a very long line waiting to place our order. The long wait made everyone difficult to get along with. When John finally made it to the head of the line, instead of just quickly giving his order so he could get served, he smiled and said, "Hi Tiffany!" He had never met this young lady. He just read her name off of her badge. He wasn't sarcastic, just polite. He spent all of ten seconds visiting with her before he placed his order.

John later explained to me the importance of a person's name to that individual. As Dale Carnegie once said, a person's name is the "sweetest and most important sound" to them. John said he has been amazed at the smiles he gets in return and the great service he receives when he simply takes the time to call a person by name. John has become a very good friend of mine since that training, and I continue to learn a lot from him and his many years of experience in working with others.

Leaders realize the power of names. Try it. Call a person by name, especially people you meet at the end of one of those long lines or an operator answering a toll free customer service line. You might just be amazed at the wonderful response you will often receive. A suitcase without a name becomes a mystery to Ron as he sorts luggage in Atlanta. Don't let people be a mystery to you. Smile and use people's names. It will help both of you quickly "arrive" at your destination.

Dollar Bill Man

SPRINGFIELD, MISSOURI

*"The things of greatest value in life
are those things that multiply when divided."*

—UNKNOWN

"Where does a dollar bill go? Send me a postcard. ddB, Rte. 1, Box 282, Highlandville, MO 65669. Have a great day!"

It was a simple message, printed thousands of times, making its way across the country and around the world. The real story is what happened to a man named "ddB" when people began to respond.

"ddB" is actually an artist in southwest Missouri named Dean Bracy. He traces his career back to a sixth grade teacher who inspired him to pursue his artistic interests. Today he works mostly in mosaics, displaying his skills in stained glass windows and tile and glass inlays. Back in the late 1990s when he began to dream of his next big project, Dean decided that the material making up the large artwork would be much different than what other artists might use. Dean wanted to make a mosaic using postcards that others would send to him.

But how would Dean get people to send him the thousands of postcards he needed? He used thousands of dollars worth of cash. Dean figured that a dollar bill comes in contact with lots of people in all areas of the country and even the world. Those bills would be the perfect way to spread his message to thousands and even millions of people. There was only one problem. He didn't have a lot of extra cash.

So, he began by getting a $10,000 loan from a friend. He made arrangements through a local bank to get that loan delivered in ten thousand new one-dollar bills from the U.S. Treasury. When the bills arrived, he then began writing his message around the edge of every single one of those bills. (He did make sure that this was not considered to be defacing money, and it is not, since he was writing around the edges of the bills.)

It took plenty of time to write those eighty-five characters on each one of those bills . . . about four hours to put the message on one hundred bills. The first ten thousand bills required two and a half months of his time before he was ready to deposit the money in his local bank. Once he made the deposit, placing the new dollars in the monetary stream, he then wrote a check for $10,000 to pay back his friend and "zero out" the account. At that point, all Dean could do was simply wait for people to respond.

Six months passed and not a single postcard arrived. Could he have really spent all that time writing on ten thousand bills and not hear back from a single person? He went to the bank to see if the bills had ever left the building and learned that the bank had sent them back to the Federal Reserve for distribution. That's where the bills had sat for over half a year. Finally, wondering if he had wasted two and half months of his time writing on all those bills, Dean began receiving postcards, mostly from the San Francisco Bay area.

From that day, the messages have never stopped coming to him in the mail. However, Dean did realize that he had a couple of factors working against him and his project. The lifespan of a dollar bill is about eighteen months. That meant the messages would slowly begin to disappear as the bills were taken out of circulation. He also realized that even though he was receiving hundreds of responses, he would need even more postcards than were coming in to complete the mosaic.

So, Dean went back to the bank and repeated the process with another ten thousand one-dollar bills. In fact, he has had to even return to the bank one final time and put a total of $30,000 worth of his messages into circulation. He hopes that will provide the number of postcard responses he needs.

Dean says this project has produced an unexpected dividend. He never realized the stories people would share as they sent their postcards to him. People don't just send a note stating where they received or spent the bill. Many times, they share the stories of their lives.

One postcard begins, "I am ninety healthy years old. I was born in a sod house in Nebraska. My daddy farmed on two sections . . ."

The stories go on and on from there, with people of all ages and all walks of life sharing their experiences with a person only known by the initials "ddB."

So far, postcards and the accompanying stories have come in from forty-nine states and many other countries. Although the mosaic will be completed with those postcards, the more valuable piece of art may just be the messages themselves. They tell the story of America and Americans.

"I learned what hope is. I see it every day," says Dean. "It's something that I certainly did not expect." We often find so much more when we simply begin to spread a message of encouragement and hope. We often forget that those messages multiply exponentially as they are passed to others.

When we stop to ponder how one individual can make a positive impact on vast numbers of people, we may just stop and realize an important lesson that Dean shared with me: "I went looking for paint and I found so much more."

Big Texan
AMARILLO, TEXAS

"The journey of a thousand miles begins with just one step."

—LAO TSE

There comes a time when you must challenge yourself to reach new heights. You must expand your abilities and dare to dream. For those who travel the lonely stretches of Interstate 40 in Oklahoma, Texas, and New Mexico, they know all too well the challenge that has been thrown before them in Amarillo. It is plastered on billboards for hundreds of miles in every direction. The challenge? Eat a seventy-two ounce steak at the Big Texan Steak Ranch in one hour.

You may have heard someone say, "I'm so hungry I could eat the whole cow." That's exactly what a cowboy said at R. J. (Bob) Lee's steakhouse back in 1960. The original eatery located on old Route 66 served up some of the best steaks to be found. When that cowboy uttered his famished cliché, Lee decided to take him up on the offer and find out exactly how much of a cow a cowboy could eat.

Lee went to work grilling steaks, serving the ranch hand plate after plate. When the evening of eating was complete, the cowboy had downed four and a half pounds of beef. Lee thought anyone who could eat that much beef in one sitting should get his or her meal for free. A promotion was born that still lives today. It's one of the biggest and best eating challenges to be found in the country.

The challenge has changed slightly from that original meal back in 1960, but the premise is still the same. The eater must first declare that he or she is going to attempt to eat the seventy-two ounce steak dinner. Notice I say "dinner," because not only must you consume the steak, you must also eat a baked potato, shrimp cocktail, dinner roll, and salad . . . just to make things fair. Not only must you eat this entire smorgasbord, you must down it in one hour or less, otherwise you pay for the meal.

After forty years of challenging customers to eat this world famous steak, over thirty-five thousand have stepped up to the plate. Just under six thousand have accomplished the feat, for an overall success percentage of about seventeen percent. Women fare far better than men in meeting the challenge, but fewer women attempt to eat the steak. Only four or five women challenge themselves to the meal each year, but about fifty percent of the women who try it achieve it.

Of course, over the years, some notable records have been achieved. For instance, the oldest person to eat the steak was a sixty-nine-year-old grandmother. On the other end of the age spectrum, the youngest to "steak" his claim was an eleven-year-old boy. Probably the most amazing record goes to Cincinnati Reds pitcher Frank Pastore, who holds the speed record. He did not need even half of his allotted hour of eating time. He checked in with an impressive yet gut wrenching time of a mere nine and a half minutes!

Although only seventeen percent of the eaters are able to consume the meal within one hour, new rules were quickly instituted in the 1960s due some particularly hungry customers. When Klondike Bill, a professional wrestler entered the establishment, he decided that one of the seventy-two ounce steaks was not enough to fill him. So, he did what any logical hungry man would do . . . he ate two complete steak dinners within the one hour time limit! Today, the rules will allow only one free meal per customer and you cannot devour more than one of those free meals every six months. Some travelers are noted to schedule their trips so that they pass through Amarillo every six months just to get their usual free meal.

Probably the most exciting part about the Big Texan and this contest is how the crowd gets involved in cheering the eaters to success. If you decide to try eating the steak, you must take a special seat by the grill. The challenger sits at a small table on a raised platform at the front of a large, open dining room. In effect, you are seated where every single customer in the place can see you. As if that weren't enough pressure, the folks at the steak ranch have conveniently placed a large digital timer right behind your seat. It steadily clicks down the remaining minutes and seconds left to consume a free meal.

Not only is the Big Texan Steak Ranch a fun place, it teaches one of the most important principles of achievement . . . something called benchmarks. It is the principle of establishing small goals within the framework of a larger and more meaningful goal.

For instance, in my work on the farm, I sometimes have to climb a tower that is over one hundred feet tall in order to check motors and grease gears on some grain handling equipment. On a windy day it can be a very scary climb, as you can feel the tower gently sway in the wind. It can become an even scarier climb if you ever decide to look down.

I know some people who simply will not climb that tower. However, I learned to overcome my fear by simply focusing on the very next wrung on the ladder and nothing else. Each wrung of the ladder is my next benchmark, a small goal helping me reach the larger goal of making it to the top of that scary tower.

Whenever a person sits down in front of the crowd at the Big Texan to take a stab at the seventy-two ounce steak, they are confronted with an overwhelming goal. However, those who are successful simply focus on taking sure and steady forkfuls of food. Each bite becomes a benchmark on the road to steakhouse immortality.

Establishing small goals or benchmarks in our lives can become important. These small goals help us remain focused on the larger task at hand. They also keep us moving in a positive direction. Most importantly, they help us simply get started on achieving a meaningful goal. Bite by bite, step by step, benchmark by benchmark . . . they are all very small steps that can lead us to eating a free steak and much, much more.

Express Mail
St. Joseph, Missouri

*"Coming together is the beginning. Keeping together is progress.
Working together is success."*

—Henry Ford

E ach rider was presented with a Bible and recited an oath of allegiance. "While I am in the employ of A. Majors, I agree not to use profane language, not to get drunk, not to gamble, not to treat animals cruelly and not to do anything else that is incompatible with the conduct of a gentleman. And I agree, if I violate any of the above conditions, to accept my discharge without any pay for my services."

When the first rider crossed the Missouri River at St. Joseph, Missouri, what lay before him was a relay race of 1,966 miles. It was a race that would last a year and a half and deliver the nation's most important messages from one coast to the other. It was the beginning of the Pony Express.

Russell, Majors, and Waddell founded the Pony Express in 1860 and although the enterprise would not make money, its attempt to deliver news at blazing speeds is still remembered today. The original stables still stand in St. Joseph, casting a shadow on Ninth Street where, ironically, UPS and FedEx trucks speed by, advertising next day delivery before 10:00 a.m..

In 1860, you used the Pony Express when your message absolutely positively had to be there in ten days or less. You paid dearly for such a speedy delivery system. Initially the price was five dollars per one-half ounce, but was later reduced to one dollar per one-half ounce. Some of the museums in the city have on display letters that were carried by the Pony Express. They attest to the high cost of using "express" mail. The paper is extremely thin and every available space on the sheet is used. If you were going to use the Pony Express, you wanted to get the most for your money.

The Pony Express relay system was remarkable. The nearly two thousand-mile course over the plains and mountains between St. Joseph and Sacramento was dotted with between 150 to 190 stations (only one of those stations is believed to remain on its original site . . . that station is near Hanover, Kansas). Riders received a new horse every ten to fifteen miles. A new rider would take the reins every seventy-five to one hundred miles. Most riders were in their late teens and twenties and were paid one hundred dollars per month. Orphans were "preferred" since the ride could be dangerous, especially in hostile Indian country.

Those were just the averages. During the history of the Pony Express, several amazing records were set. Bob Haslam once rode an incredible 370-mile shift without a break. The youngest rider was Charlie Miller, who was a mere eleven years old. The fastest trip was seven days and seventeen hours from Ft. Kearney, Nebraska, to Placerville, California (the two ends of the telegraph line at the time). The riders were carrying a copy of Lincoln's Inaugural Address.

But as 1860 turned into 1861, the telegraph poles from the east and west grew ever closer, narrowing the gap that a message had to gallop. Eventually those ends of the telegraph line would meet on October 24, 1861. The event meant the end of the Pony Express. Urgent messages could now be sent in seconds instead of days, though freight still used what was known as the central route—the route the

Pony Express followed—and later the transcontinental railroad and today's Interstate 80 did as well.

Financially, the Pony Express failed. The owners lost $500,000 dollars on the venture. However, in one and a half years, only one mail delivery was ever lost. The team of ponies and riders performed their jobs just as designed. Messages were transported, station-to-station, as quickly as possible, over a sometimes dangerous course of almost two thousand miles.

That great relay race remains as an example to us today. A well-designed network of stations, men, supplies, and horses was able to accomplish swift mail delivery. Too often, we minimize the importance of the network of people we meet every day. We can learn from everyone, and we have something we can give to everyone as well. President Woodrow Wilson once said, "I use not only all the brains I have, but all that I can borrow." He was referring to the network of people who provided him the information to run a country. It was a network of relationships he built over time. Never underestimate the value of your "network." It can become an express route to accomplishing great things.

*"You gain strength, courage, and confidence by every
experience by which you really stop to look fear in the face.
You are able to say to yourself, 'I lived through this horror.
I can take the next thing that comes along.'"*

—Eleanor Roosevelt

When Weldon Hamilton pulled into Manila Harbor on the twentieth of November in 1941, he never imagined the struggle he would experience for the next three years. It would be a journey that would require the highest levels of strength and courage possessed by men.

Manila was an exciting place in 1941, a vibrant city preparing for war. In fact, just over a week later, on November 29, the U.S. knew the enemy would soon be on the way. Weldon had only been on the islands for a few days and was already headed to Del Carmen Field. His commander informed the squadron, "There would be war within seventy-two hours." He was right.

The Japanese initially attacked nearby Clark Field, destroying runways and most of the U.S. planes based there. Weldon meanwhile stayed at Del Carmen until Christmas Day. He, too, endured Japanese bombing there and vividly remembers their planes lining up to attack the field. "You're thinkin', 'Oh boy, if they start droppin' them now they'll run out before they get to us. If they wait long enough they'll miss us and go on over us.' But when you see that it looks like they're going to get you, you cram your head just as far into the dirt as you can and it feels like a giant walkin' up on you."

Weldon survived those bombings during December and by Christmas Day Radio Manila reported that U.S. troops were holding on all fronts. That sounded like good news. Soon a captain in a jeep came by and Weldon asked him about the news report. "That means we're retreating as fast as they're advancing," the captain said. With that, it was time for the troops to retreat as well, heading toward Orani at the mouth of the Bataan Peninsula to make a last stand there.

Weldon eventually retreated into an area just across from the island of Corregidor at the tip of the Bataan Peninsula then on to Agaloma Bay for beach defense. Even this remote place would not escape enemy attack. On the night of January 22, 1942, about 750 Japanese marines landed on the beach. Although the Americans and Filipinos were able to hold back that first landing, in time the Japanese would overwhelm the smaller retreating force. The final surrender didn't come until April 9. Actually, the Japanese accepted no formal surrender terms. The American troops were simply told to wait for further instructions.

There wasn't a single march of thousands of U.S. troops that can be called the "Bataan Death March." Weldon explained that it was several small marches made up of different groups of troops. However, the treatment was the same for all.

"If you fell out, they killed you. If you couldn't go, that was just too bad. Guys would say 'I can't go any further,' and they would just fall down and they would be killed just like that." It is estimated that about ten thousand soldiers died along the march route. In all, the march lasted about twelve days and covered approximately seventy miles. During that time the prisoners received little, if any, food and Weldon said you just had to scramble to find water.

Those who survived the march also had to endure a suffocating ride in a boxcar to reach Camp O'Donnell, the prisoner-of-war camp.

Another twenty-five thousand men are believed to have died within the first two months of their stay at the camp. Upon arrival at O'Donnell, the Japanese commander of the POW camp addressed the prisoners: "We are enemies, we shall always be enemies . . . from generation unto generation, even unto hundreds of years. You think you are lucky to have escaped with your lives? I tell you, the lucky ones are already dead. I am interested in only one thing, how many people die every day." That was the truth. Some times as many as one thousand men died a day.

Weldon and the other prisoners were soon moved to the prisoner of war camp at Cabanatuan. He remained there for about two years. The details of his imprisonment are hard to comprehend. His body was so weak from dysentery that he could not even lift his foot over a doorsill. Much of those two years of time was spent in the hospital ward at Cabanatuan where he slowly recovered. To his knowledge, he was the only man to leave his ward alive.

By the summer of 1944, Weldon had regained some of his strength and he got the medics to clear him as recovered from dysentery. That clearance allowed him to volunteer to go to Japan and work in a prison camp there. It took sixty-two days to sail from the Philippines to Japan. The ships were horribly overcrowded and Weldon received a cup of water and one cup of rice every day. He was fortunate not to lose his life to the hands of his own soldiers. American submarines sank many ships that made those journeys. Of course, they had no way of knowing who or what might be on the Japanese ships.

Weldon was put to work in a coal mine under the ocean and spent the remainder of his POW life in prison camp number seventeen. Although life was difficult, Weldon liked the mine. The temperatures were comfortable and there were plenty of places to hide. The Americans bombed the camp repeatedly as the end of the war neared. He remembers that many American POWs yelled, "Burn it down, burn it down" to their fellow American pilots dropping the bombs on the camp. Weldon was more realistic as he saw his housing go up in flames. He wondered, "What are we going to do next winter?" Still, he was glad that U.S. forces seemed to be making headway in the war.

Weldon did see the towering mushroom cloud from the bomb that was dropped on Nagasaki. However, the POWs had no idea what the explosion might have been. Soon, Japanese soldiers told the Americans that there would be a "vacation" day from the mines. Finally, on August 14, 1945, the Japanese commander of the camp addressed the prisoners and stated, "Hostilities have ceased. Let us all be friends." The U.S. troops thought that was a "pretty cute" way to call an end to a horrendous three-year stay in prison. It was as if they had been vacationing relatives and were now heading back to their own homes.

Weldon has written a book titled *Late Summer of 1941 and My War with Japan*. It gives great insights into life as a prisoner of war during World War II. As I sat with Weldon and listened to him share his story, I wondered, "How does a man endure such treatment and survive?" Weldon says that many things were totally out of his control, yet he did learn plenty from his experience that he shares with others today.

"They admired courage over everything. They would beat you and beat you until you couldn't move. The whole idea was, no matter how hard they beat you, never let them see that it bothered you," he says. "Man can endure the most horrible things and still come out whole on the other side."

Weldon's book is a testament to courage and determination. Few of us may ever be asked to endure so much for our country or our beliefs. Yet, we have the example of American POWs that reveal to us the power of such qualities. These are the traits that help men and women survive and succeed in the face of death and to achieve what we only dream.

They Will Come

Dyersville, Iowa

"Destiny is no matter of chance. It is a matter of choice. It is not a thing to be waited for, it is a thing to be achieved."

—William Jennings Bryan

"This field, this game, is a part of our past, Ray. It reminds us of all that once was good and could be again. Oh . . . people will come, Ray. People will most definitely come."

When James Earl Jones delivered those famous lines to a farmer named Ray Kinsella (played by Kevin Costner) in the movie *Field of Dreams,* no one may have realized exactly how long people might keep coming to that field. Just as the ending credits of the film kept rolling, cars just kept rolling down the lane. What's amazing is that long after those credits quit scrolling, cars have never stopped driving down this farm lane near Dyersville, Iowa. It's a place that made for baseball magic on the big screen, and it still creates magic every summer on the Lansing farm.

My car, too, made that drive down the farm lane to behold the field and learn more about its amazing story. Long before there was ever a baseball field here, there was a family farm. That farm and the family who owns it, the Lansings, have been here for nearly a century now, with the land being passed from generation to generation. Farming is still the everyday, year-round chore that takes place at the Lansing farmstead.

But back in 1988, the search was on for Universal Studios to find the right farm from which to film a new baseball movie. The movie makers made their way to over 250 farms from Georgia to Canada before the director saw the Lansing farm and immediately knew this was the perfect backdrop.

If you've seen the movie, you may remember that Ray Kinsella hears a voice coming from his cornfield that beckons, "If you build it, they will come." He eventually figures out that "it" is a baseball field. To the astonishment of his neighbors, he plows up his corn and begins to build the field, simply trusting that players will come just as the voice says.

In real life, there was almost not a corn crop to plow under during the summer of 1988. That year saw one of the worst droughts in history hit the Midwest. Becky Lansing, whose husband planted the crop that spring, explained to me that the movie crew didn't fully comprehend the business of farming.

One day during the height of the drought the director came to her husband and said, "Don, if there's no corn, there's no movie."

He simply replied, "Welcome to farming."

It wasn't as if Universal could just move down the road and find a well-watered corn field with another perfect farmstead backdrop. They had to do something to make the Lansing crop come to life. Growing corn for Universal Studios can be a little different than raising a crop for just about anyone else. With the movie on the line, Universal decided to dam a small creek running through the Lansing's farm. The small reservoir that resulted was used to irrigate the surrounding corn fields.

It worked too well. The parched Iowa corn used the new-found moisture to make an unexpected growth spurt. In fact, the corn was too tall by the time Universal was ready to film Kevin Costner walking through the fields for the opening scene of the movie.

Unknown to viewers, Costner is actually walking through those fields on a twelve-inch high platform. Otherwise the crop would have covered him completely.

Once the field is built, players do magically appear. Famous baseball athletes who have passed, such as Shoeless Joe Jackson, make their way to play on the new field. They simply walk out of Ray's corn field and onto the outfield grass.

The film is truly a journey for Costner's character, who eventually is reunited with his late father to play on the field that he has built. The *Field of Dreams* is about much more than baseball. Many of the characters in the movie are able to recapture special moments that passed them by during their lifetimes. Today, for many of the visitors who travel to this field, it serves as a reflection on their own lives . . . an examination of what was and what could have been.

It took fifteen weeks to shoot the scenes at the Lansing farm. The contract with Universal stated that the baseball field was to be returned to a corn field when filming was complete. However, Don Lansing and his family had fallen in love with that field and saw the potential of the site as a tourist destination. So, the field and the farm remains as it looked back in 1988 for the movie.

In the movie, Terrance Mann (James Earl Jones) told Ray Kinsella, "People will most definitely come." They didn't realize how true that statement would be in real life. Each year fifty-five thousand or more visitors may come to this field. Becky says there is "a lot of magic" that takes place here on summer days. "There's a pick-up game that goes on all day long. People sit in the bleachers and dream. They walk the bases and they sit under our evergreen trees and bring a picnic lunch. They reconcile, they dream, they think about fulfilled and unfulfilled wishes. It's magic all day long."

Visitors can bring their own bats, baseballs, and gloves (these aren't supplied due to insurance reasons). In a sense, the game that began on the big screen continues today. It is truly a special place for many.

Becky does like seeing visitors enjoy their famous diamond. However, she hopes they do not come here for the wrong reasons. She explains, "People sometimes come to the Field of Dreams looking for something. I would respectfully say to those people, 'We want you to come here, but sit in your backyard for five or ten minutes and see if you can't find that peaceful place all by yourself. Certainly we want you to come here and feel what we feel, but remember that peace exists no matter where you are as long as you are mindful and soulful of what it is you're looking for.'"

Some people spend all their time searching for a special place that will suddenly transform their lives. They often never find that special place because they fail to go to the very first place they should look . . . inside their selves. I'm not talking about becoming "your own God," taking philosophy classes, or relying on yourself for all of life's answers. I'm simply talking about looking at the wonderful gifts God has given you and then setting your mind to use your abilities to improve yourself and help others every day. That's what turns dreams into realities.

Certainly there are times when we feel a little lost and we regret not taking advantage of opportunities earlier in life. However, we each can begin to make choices and changes that will positively impact our lives today and in the future. What we will find is that after all the journeys we have taken and all the lessons we have learned, the application begins with each one of us right in our very own homes. No, there is not a place we can go that will do that for us. It begins with us.